Drawing is a Class Act

Years 3–4

Meg Fabian

'In learning to draw (unlike learning to write) you learn to look.'
'Then you teach yourself to see and to feel what you see.'
David Hockney
from the forward to Draw: How to Master the Art by Jeffrey Camp

Acknowledgements

I would like to thank:
Andrew Riley, Primary Phase Adviser and erstwhile Headteacher at two of the primary schools where I have taught art, for his help, advice, encouragement and inspiration not only in the initial stages of this book but also during all the time we worked together.

Dr Aubrey Wilson for his sterling advice and support.

Chris Wightman and Phil Creek, the Devon Curriculum Services Art Advisers, for all the art courses they have run, when I have turned up exhausted and jaded and left enthused and full of ideas.

I would also like to thank the following primary schools for their permission to include in the publication examples of work by children in their schools. This work has been done over a number of years. Wherever work is named, permission was sought for inclusion.

Primary schools

Berrynarbor
Burrington
Chawleigh
Clovelly
East Worlington
Filleigh
Witheridge
Winkleigh

Individual pupils

Alex Lyons-Martin
Ben Burgess-Farrant
Billie Reay
Charlotte Rice
Chris Dennis
Christopher Burrige
Daisy Burt
Daisy Perham
Hannah Clark
Heidi Green
Hettie Pearson
Hugh White
Jack Perham
Jade Tanton
James Chapman
Jordan Clark
Jordan Prowse
Joshua Lee
Lemar Bradford
Matthew Tyzak
Melissa Peddar
Melissa Orton
Oliver Coulham
Raymond Penfold
Tara Perham
Thomas Ellis
Thomas Gatehouse
Wesley Knowler

The publishers and author would like to thank the following for permission to reproduce artwork in this book (page nos. given in brackets):

Design and Artists Copyright Society (DACS) (133 bottom right, 134, 143 bottom right); Kunsthistorisches Museum, Vienna (74, 139); Museum of Amsterdam (24, 130, 143 left); Tate, London 2005 (25, 90, 131, 133, 134, 135, 143 right); Sarah Wimperis (132); Windsor Castle (18, 129)

Brilliant Publications, 1 Church View, Sparrow Hall Farm, Edlesborough, Dunstable, Bedfordshire LU6 2ES
Tel: 01525 229720
Fax: 01525 229725
e-mail: sales@brilliantpublications.co.uk
website: www.brilliantpublications.co.uk
The name Brilliant Publications and the logo are registered trademarks.
Written by Meg Fabian
Illustrations supplied by class pupils (see list above)
Front cover design by Lynda Murray
Cover illustrations by Christopher Burrige, Heidi Green, Jade Tanton, Tara Perham

ISBN 1 903853 61 3 (978-1-903853-61-0)
Printed in the UK by RPM Print & Design
10 9 8 7 6 5 4 3 2 1

Forward

Many of the examples in this book have been developed through collaborative work across a number of small primary schools in Devon. The schools worked with Meg Fabian over a period of two years. This collaborative work, involving a specialist with a passion for her subject, was instrumental in raising children's standards and confidence in drawing. Teachers also benefited from gaining knowledge and skills to improve their own understanding and teaching of drawing.

It became clear during the collaborative work that teachers needed the guidance and encouragement of a subject specialist: this is what this book provides for all teachers. By clearly setting out the development of drawing skills from the beginning, offering guidance on progression in learning and providing ideas to support classroom activities, this book is exactly what busy primary teachers need.

The schools involved in this innovative collaborative work believed in the importance of raising standards in art and the impact this has on the promotion of high standards in other subjects of the curriculum and, importantly, in children's self-esteem and confidence. The schools reflected this belief in practice and dedicated a higher proportion of time to the teaching of art. They also recognized that, to achieve high standards in art, the class teacher may need support in identifying the developmental stages of drawing.

This is where this book will be an invaluable resource.

David Chaplin
Lead Adviser
Devon Curriculum Services

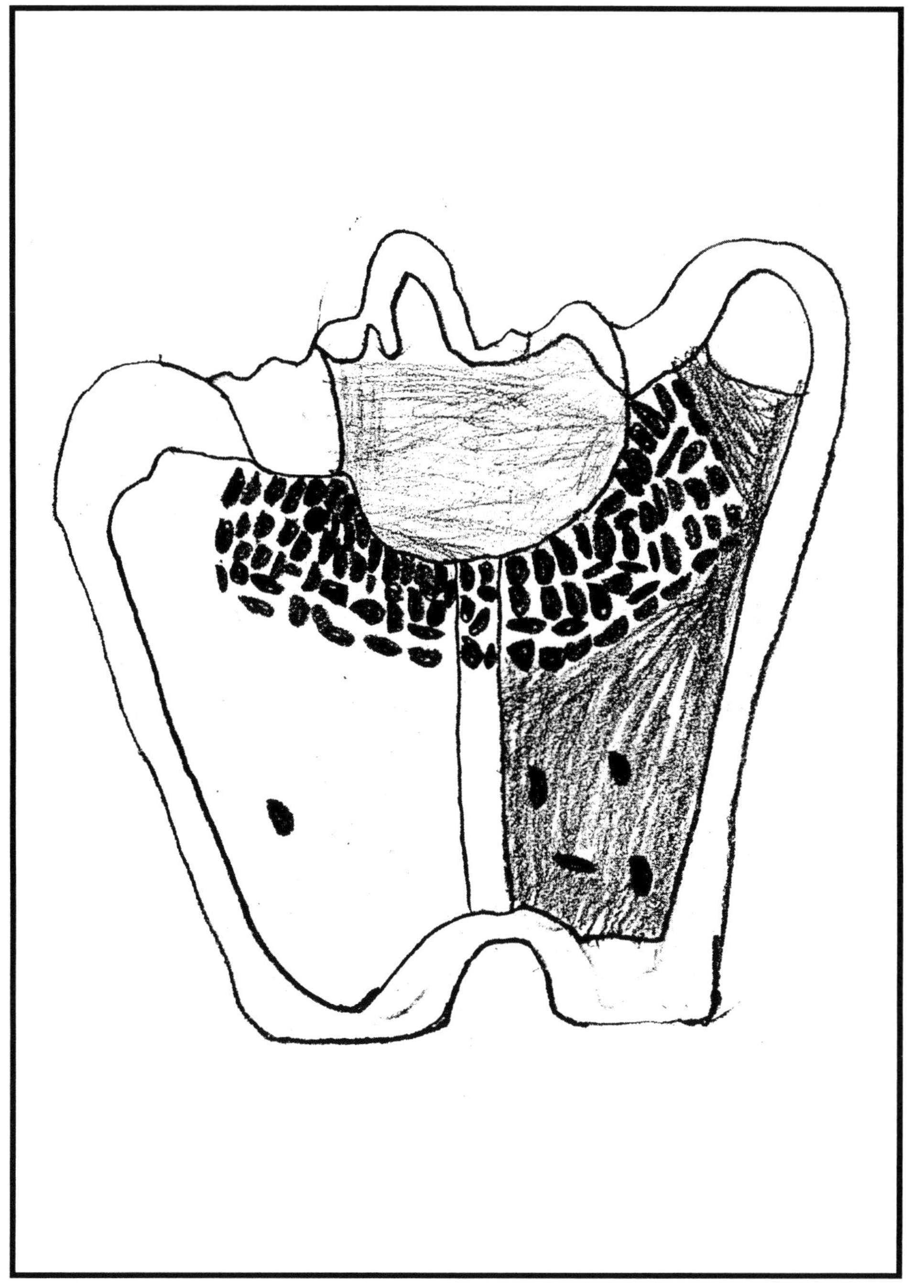

Year 3 child's drawing of inside of a pepper

Contents

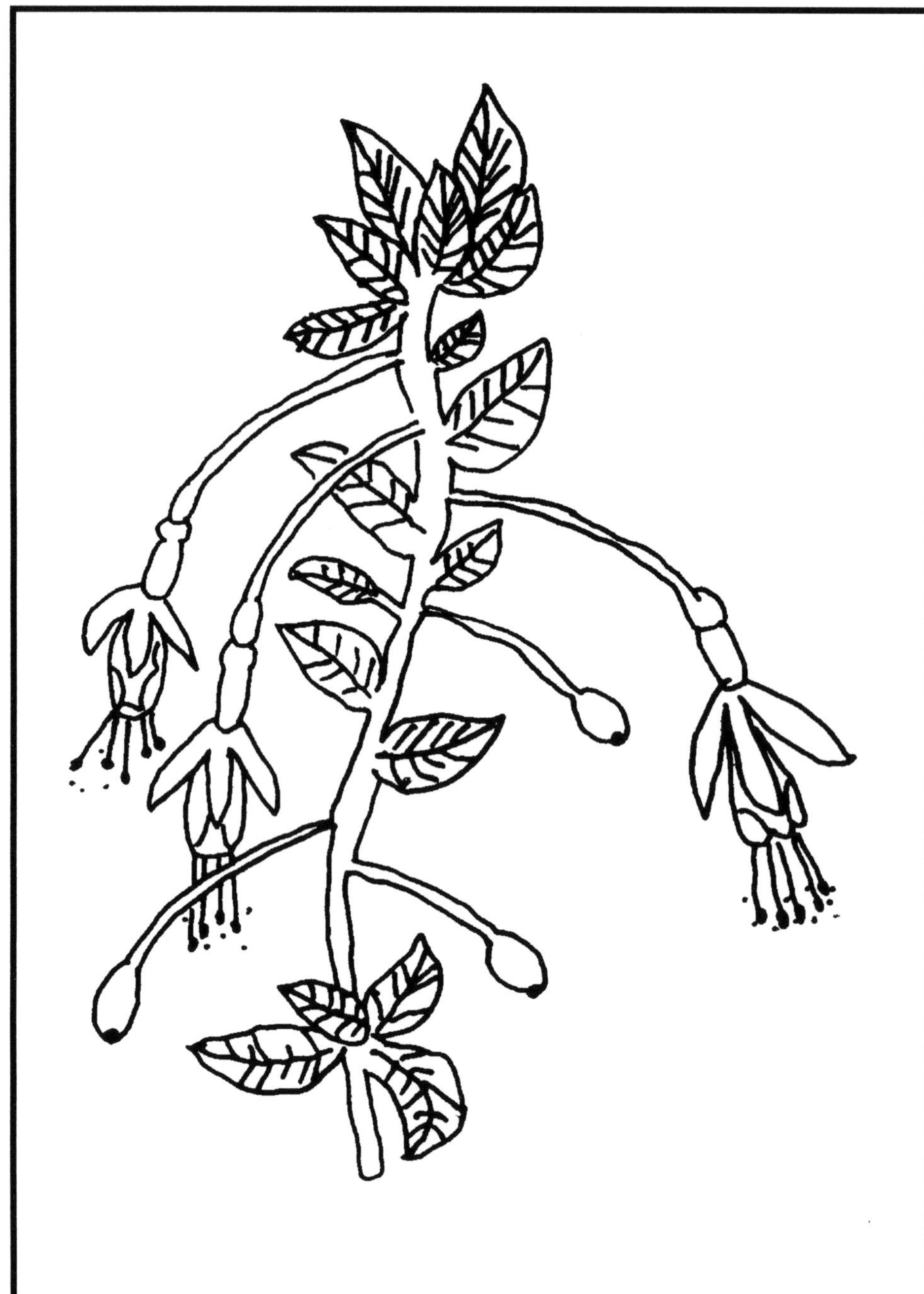

Melissa Peddar, Year 3

A skills-based approach to drawing

The aim of this book is to support non-specialist art teachers working in primary schools. It is intended for teachers who say, *'I want to help my children get better at drawing but I don't know how,'* and to help teachers respond confidently to all those children who say *'I'm rubbish at drawing.'*

This book is designed to be easily accessed. It is intended that teachers can glance at a page, read the title, look at the example of pupils' work and know what to do without reading all the text. Teachers wanting further information can read the page.

Each lesson plan includes:

- Lesson title indicating the skill or technique being covered
- Logo indicating the type of lesson:

- Time needed to complete lesson
- Resources
- Links to National Curriculum programmes of study
- Introduction to pupils
- Practical activity
- Examples of pupils' work.

Many lessons also include:

- Background information necessary to deliver the lesson
- Examples of works of art that illustrate the use of the skills being taught.

Some lessons include:

- A photocopiable worksheet
- Possible pitfalls.

How the skills-based approach works

The principle of this book is that the skills and techniques covered should be used for a purpose as soon as possible. It is important that children have the opportunity to use their skills in a drawing context.

For this reason a 'Using skill' lesson follows each 'Key skill' or 'Skill' lesson throughout the book. For example, when children have learned the skills for using line with charcoal they can then use these skills to draw school buildings, windswept trees, etc. This also gives the teacher a clear focus for assessment.

The drawing subject could be linked to another appropriate topic, for example if the local environment is being studied in history or geography, then this is an excellent opportunity to apply the art skills to drawing landscape.

For some lessons it is recommended that teachers demonstrate or model basic techniques. This generally involves nothing more challenging than drawing light and dark lines using charcoal or drawing a cube on the board. Paper can be fixed to the board with Blu-tac® for demonstrating. Where paper is necessary for teacher modelling, it is mentioned in the resources list for that lesson.

Many of the skills exercises will result in a piece of work that is visually pleasing in its own right. Children will produce something they can be proud of. This factor has been deliberately built in. Very often, once the skill has been taught, the pieces of work can be adapted or mounted to produce a stunning piece of artwork that can be displayed to great effect. There are some good examples of this in the 'Playing around with line' lesson (see page 33). If it makes the children feel *'Wow, I did that'*, it will increase their confidence, their self-esteem and their willingness to take the next step.

The skills-based approach doesn't inhibit creativity; it helps children to know how to create certain effects. If they have increased control and understanding of the different media, they will be able to experiment with more confidence and be empowered to express themselves.

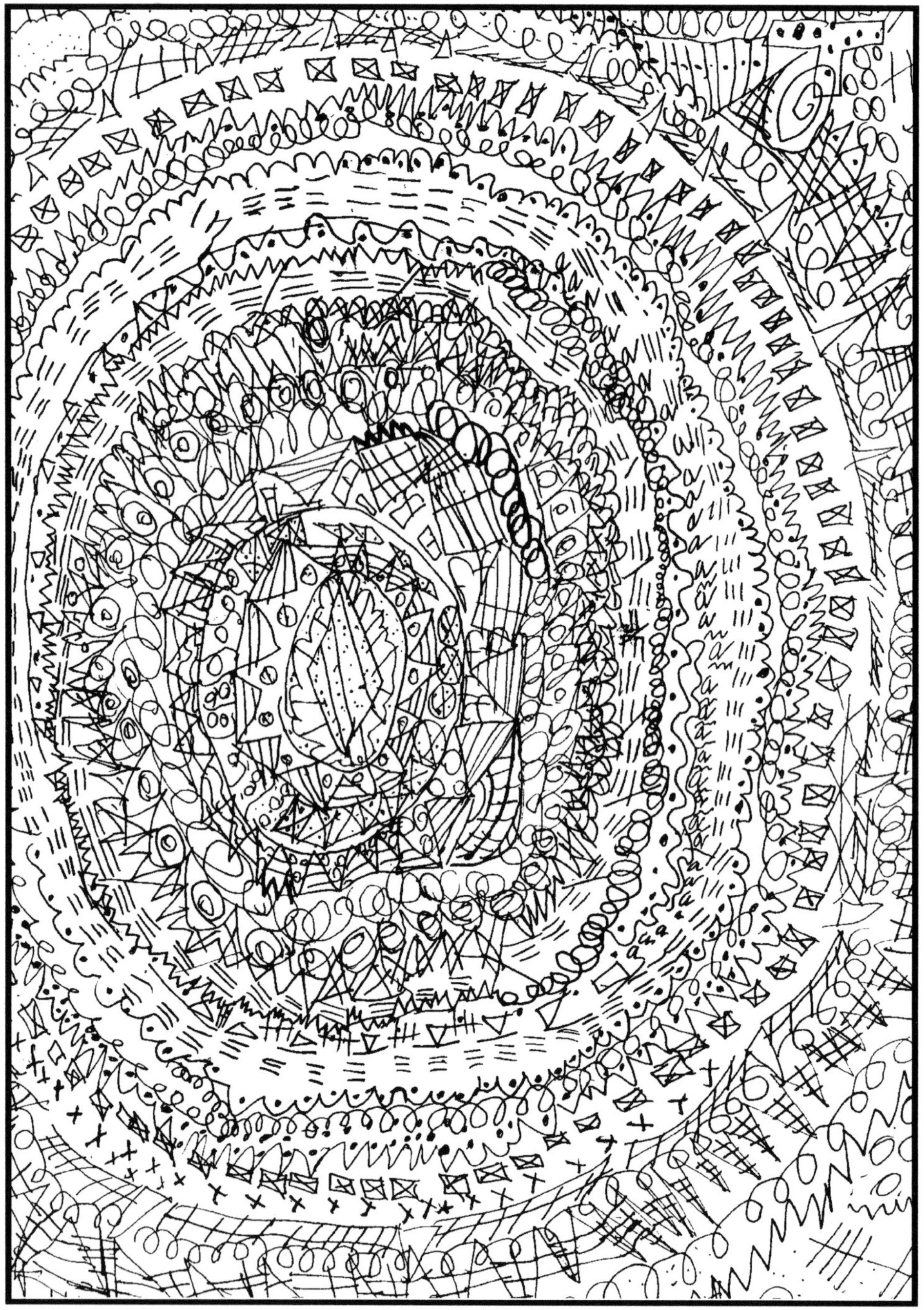

Year 3 child's pen drawing

What the book covers

This book covers all the National Curriculum programmes of study related to drawing. The programmes of study are listed for each lesson.

The book has chapters on line, tone, texture, pattern, looking, figures and faces, and chalk and charcoal. The contents pages clearly set out the lessons for each chapter, giving the type of lesson and approximate time needed for each. There is also a chapter on evaluation and assessment.

The book:

- ❐ Clearly sets out the progression of skills
- ❐ Has lesson plans for lower juniors which can be adapted easily for small schools with mixed age ranges, or single-age classes where there is a wide range of ability
- ❐ Has examples of pupils' artwork showing the skills at each stage
- ❐ Gives examples of how the skills can be applied (children are more motivated when they can see clearly how the skill can be used)
- ❐ Has responses to works of art integrated into each unit
- ❐ Has photocopiable reproductions of works of art and other photocopiable resources (all of which are to be found at the back of the book).

It is not expected that all the lessons will be delivered. Teachers can teach one, some, or most of the lessons. However, if there is very limited time, then it is suggested that just the key skill lessons are taught.

These lessons are marked with this symbol. The key skill lessons appear in bold on the contents pages.

Other books in the series

This book is one of a series of three. The other books in the series cover Key Stage 1 and upper Key Stage 2.

Years 1–2 ISBN 1 903853 60 5 (978-1-903853-60-3)

Years 5–6 ISBN 1 903853 62 1 (978-1-903853-62-7)

About drawing

Dictionary derivation of 'to draw':

- ❐ Old High German Tragen
- ❐ Old High Norse Draga
- ❐ Old High Goth Gadragon
- ❐ Old English Dragon

The various ways we use the word 'drawing' are fascinating, at once connected and yet different:

- ❐ To draw out
- ❐ To be drawn along
- ❐ To be drawn into
- ❐ To draw alongside
- ❐ To draw from experience
- ❐ To draw closer …

'It is the *draw closer* that is the most interesting. When I am drawing, I become totally involved, I concentrate intensely, become more closely involved with what I am drawing. There comes a point when I am almost at one with my subject, I feel all my senses are engaged. I miss nothing.'

Meg Fabian, the author

So many adults feel that they cannot draw; this is perhaps because they have never been taught to draw.

'Most adults in the Western world do not progress in art skills beyond the level of the development they reached at nine or ten. In most mental and physical activities individuals' skills change and develop as they grow to adulthood. The development of drawing skills, however, seems to halt unaccountably at an early age for most people. This could be because drawing is not a vital skill for survival in our culture, but reading and writing are.'

Betty Edwards, Drawing on the Right Side of the Brain

Learning to draw is something that never stops. Children are surprised when they hear that artists go on learning and getting better all their lives, that they never consider they have stopped developing as artists.

Drawing is surrounded by mystique. It is commonly imagined that the few who can perform its magical rites have been invested with a divine gift – but actually anyone can learn to draw.

'From the age of six, I had a mania for drawing the form of things. At seventy-five I learned a little about the real structure of nature. At ninety I shall penetrate the mystery of things; at a hundred I shall have reached a marvellous stage; and when I am a hundred and ten, everything I do, be it a dot or a line, will be alive.'

Written at the age of 75 by Owakio Rojin, an old man mad about drawing (from Betty Edwards, Drawing on the Right Side of the Brain)

There are many purposes for drawing, for example recording, expressing, communicating and analyzing.

This book is about exploring the media and elements.

Jack Perham, Year 4

About looking

The key to drawing is in the looking. For this reason a separate chapter is devoted to it.

Children find it hard to believe that as artists their eyes are more important than their hands. The skills covered in the Looking chapter will help them understand how and why this is true. They will be guided not only to look closely but to look with purpose and to develop different ways of looking.

'In developing children's ability to see and understand various visual situations you produce a storehouse of ideas that can be used in countless different ways.'
Ian Simpson, Drawing, Seeing and Observation

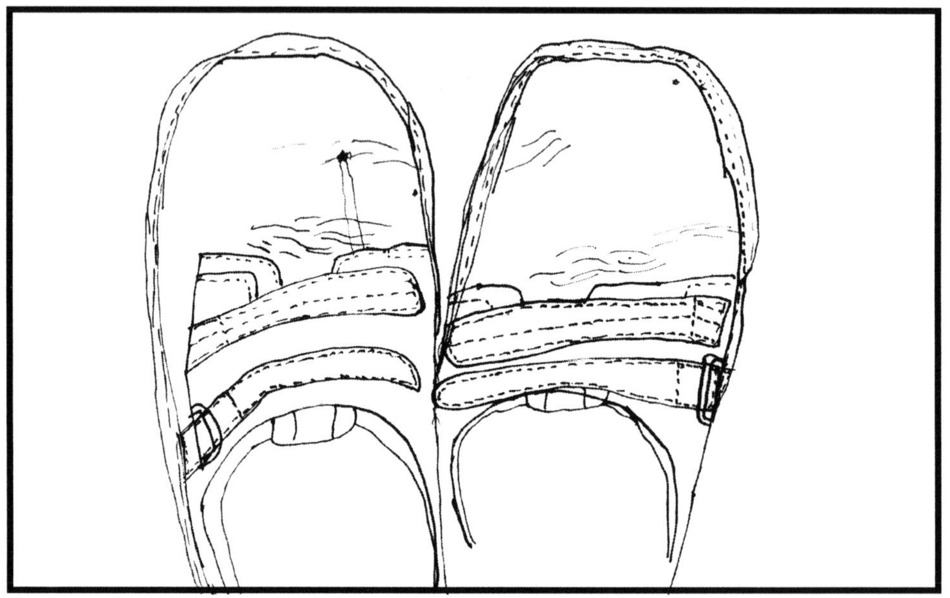

Oliver Coulham, Year 3 (drawn looking down at crossed feet)

Moving on from Key Stage 1

The most difficult task children have to overcome in drawing is that they live in a three-dimensional world which they are trying to represent on a two-dimensional surface.

Schema

When they are younger they solve this problem by drawing symbols or schema. Shapes rarely overlap each other and subject matter is surrounded by space. The bottom of the paper serves as the ground and most subjects are drawn facing the viewer. Heads are often round and way too big, the mouth is a curved line, feet are too small and point the same way.

Examples of Year 3–4 schema

There is nothing wrong with schema as long as children don't get 'fixed' in the schematic stage and become unable to move on. Children often need to use schema to quickly create storyboards, to record ideas or to illustrate work from another curriculum area.

At Years 3 and 4 observational drawing can be developed alongside narrative drawing as both have their place – just as notes or plans for written work exist alongside extended writing. Teachers can introduce closer looking with younger or less able pupils through talking about, touching and describing the subject matter. This is the foundation for engaging their looking and it will feed into their drawings gradually.

This next stage of children's drawing development is probably the hardest. Children need to move gradually away from their comfortable schema, look longer and harder and think more carefully before they draw.

For a while their spontaneity in drawing seems to go. This is a crucial stage in drawing in which children need strategies to help them succeed. Some children will want to give up, they can become frustrated when their drawings don't 'go right'. Their drawings seem to lack the charm of younger children, but are not yet as competent as their elders.

It is at this point that many children first gain the notion that they are 'no good at art'. This idea often stays with them through life. This is tragic. If they are given structured support and some tips and techniques to help them through this stage, they will quickly realize that they can make good progress and achieve very satisfying results.

Being able to draw well brings considerable peer approval and gives increased confidence to young artists, but they need to understand that it will involve having a serious attitude, applying themselves and perseverance. However, it may not be easy.

Charlotte Rice, Year 4

Range of media

To deliver the lessons in this book you will need (absolute basics are in bold):

❒ One set of drawing pencils H to 8B for display
❒ B, **2B** and 4B **pencils**
❒ **Fine line pens (tip size 0.4 mm)**
❒ Permanent pens, medium tip
❒ Permanent pens, broad tip (round tips are more manageable than chisel)
❒ Erasers
❒ **Charcoal, medium thickness**
❒ **White chalk** or white chalky pastel
❒ **Fixative** (see Glossary – cheap hairspray can be used)
❒ **Oil pastels**
❒ Brusho (powdered watercolour)
❒ Coloured pencils, art quality
❒ Crayons
❒ Felt tips
❒ Ball-point pens
❒ Graphite
❒ Conté crayons (soft pastels)
❒ Sketchbooks (A4)
❒ Viewfinders (see Glossary and page 74–75)
❒ Magnifying glasses
❒ Mirrors (plastic)
❒ Cartridge paper (see Glossary)

Starting-out kit:
Tip: buy good-quality media, topping up when you can. Gradually extend range a little at a time.

- ❒ B and 4B pencils (add 2B when you can)
- ❒ Fine line pens (tip size 0.4 mm), water-based
- ❒ Permanent pens, broad tip (add medium tip when you can)
- ❒ Charcoal, medium thickness
- ❒ Fixative (see Glossary)
- ❒ Oil pastels (extend range of colours later)
- ❒ Art pastels (chalky)
- ❒ Art quality coloured pencils. (These are expensive so could be left until budget allows. The water colour pencils are the most versatile as they can be used in two ways: as coloured pencils and as a form of water colours.)
- ❒ Sketchbooks, A4 – for more information see page 14
- ❒ Viewfinders made from cut black sugar paper (replace with card or corrugated plastic when you can)

'Drawing is the discipline by which I constantly rediscover the world. I have learned that what I have never drawn I have never seen, and when I start drawing an ordinary thing, I realize how extraordinary it is, sheer miracle.'
Frederick Frank, The Zen of Seeing

'For me drawing is a kind of thinking, but it is also about the medium.'
Antony Gormley, sculptor of The Angel of the North (from his book, Drawing)

A well-resourced art cupboard could have:

- ❒ H, B, 2B, 4B, 6B pencils
- ❒ Fine line pens (tip size 0.3 mm or 0.4 mm), water-based
- ❒ Fine (tip size 0.4 mm), medium and broad permanent pens
- ❒ Charcoal, thin and thick
- ❒ Fixative
- ❒ Oil pastels, 25 colours, bright and subtle, extra white and black
- ❒ Art pastels, good range of colours, including landscape colours
- ❒ Conté crayons (soft pastels), black, white, earth colours, sepia, burned sienna, etc.
- ❒ Good-quality crayons, some sets in people colours
- ❒ Art quality coloured pencils, landscape and portrait sets
- ❒ Water colour pencils
- ❒ Graphite
- ❒ Metallic crayons
- ❒ Metallic pens – fine and broad
- ❒ Sketchbooks with heavy quality paper
- ❒ Clipboards for outside drawing
- ❒ Black plastic viewfinders
- ❒ Magnifying glasses with flexible necks that clamp onto desk
- ❒ Lamps with flexible necks
- ❒ Collection of reproductions of works of art, filed according to topic or subject, or QCA art documents
- ❒ Collection of artefacts for drawing (see list on page 69)
- ❒ Collection of CD-Roms featuring works of art for use on computer and white boards

Sketchbooks

'Drawing sketches is like planting seeds in order to get pictures later.'
Van Gogh, in a letter to his brother Theo (from The Letters)

Most artists use a sketchbook. It is a vital part of their equipment used to collect visual information and to record ideas and feelings. On his death Picasso left 178 sketchbooks, containing a huge variety of ideas recorded over a period of 60 years. A page from one of Vincent van Gogh's sketchbooks appears on page 143.

It is a good idea for children to see artists' sketchbooks and to hear how they use them. This could be part of a school visit by a practising artist. If this is not possible, members of a local art group would probably be willing to visit the school and allow the children to see their sketchbooks and answer children's questions about how they are used.

Throughout this book it is suggested that children do the work outlined in each lesson directly in their sketchbooks. Sketchbooks are listed in the resources list for most lessons. When it is not possible to work directly in the sketchbooks (for example, in the Chalk and charcoal chapter the drawings are executed on mid-tone sugar paper), the drawings could be stuck into the sketchbooks later.

A sketchbook is a wonderful record of a child's development as a young artist. Being able to look back at their work and see their progression raises children's self-esteem.

Teachers can write comments in sketchbooks just as they would in other subject books. Comments should be specific, for example: *'I like the way you have used different kinds of lines in this drawing,'* or *'I can tell that you were looking very carefully when you drew this.'*

Sketchbooks should be started in Key Stage 1, and carry on through the school. They should be at least A4 and of reasonable quality paper. Slightly bigger than A4 is ideal, as A4 paper can be stuck in without any overlaps. Work may often be done on loose paper and stuck in later, perhaps because the artwork is going to be displayed or work has been done on different types or colours of paper.

The sketchbook paper needs to be thick enough to take paint, as the sketchbooks should be used across the whole art curriculum. The paper should have slight texture, as very smooth paper is not ideal for pencil.

The covers should be stiff enough for the children to lean on when drawing outside. Hard-backed sketchbooks are excellent and can last for years but they are expensive and very heavy.

'A day passed without drawing is a day wasted.'
Antony Gormley, sculptor of The Angel of the North (from his book, Drawing)

Sketchbooks can be used for different purposes:

- ❒ Collecting visual information
- ❒ Capturing an image
- ❒ Planning
- ❒ Trying out new skills
- ❒ Experimenting with media
- ❒ Visual storytelling
- ❒ Note-taking
- ❒ Designing
- ❒ Describing
- ❒ Storing ideas
- ❒ Recording research
- ❒ Recording investigations
- ❒ Recording responses

Sketchbooks are:

- ❒ A record of achievement
- ❒ A record of development

They can be used for assessment:

- ❒ Self-evaluation
- ❒ For reporting to parents
- ❒ As evidence

Sketchbooks are a source of inspiration.

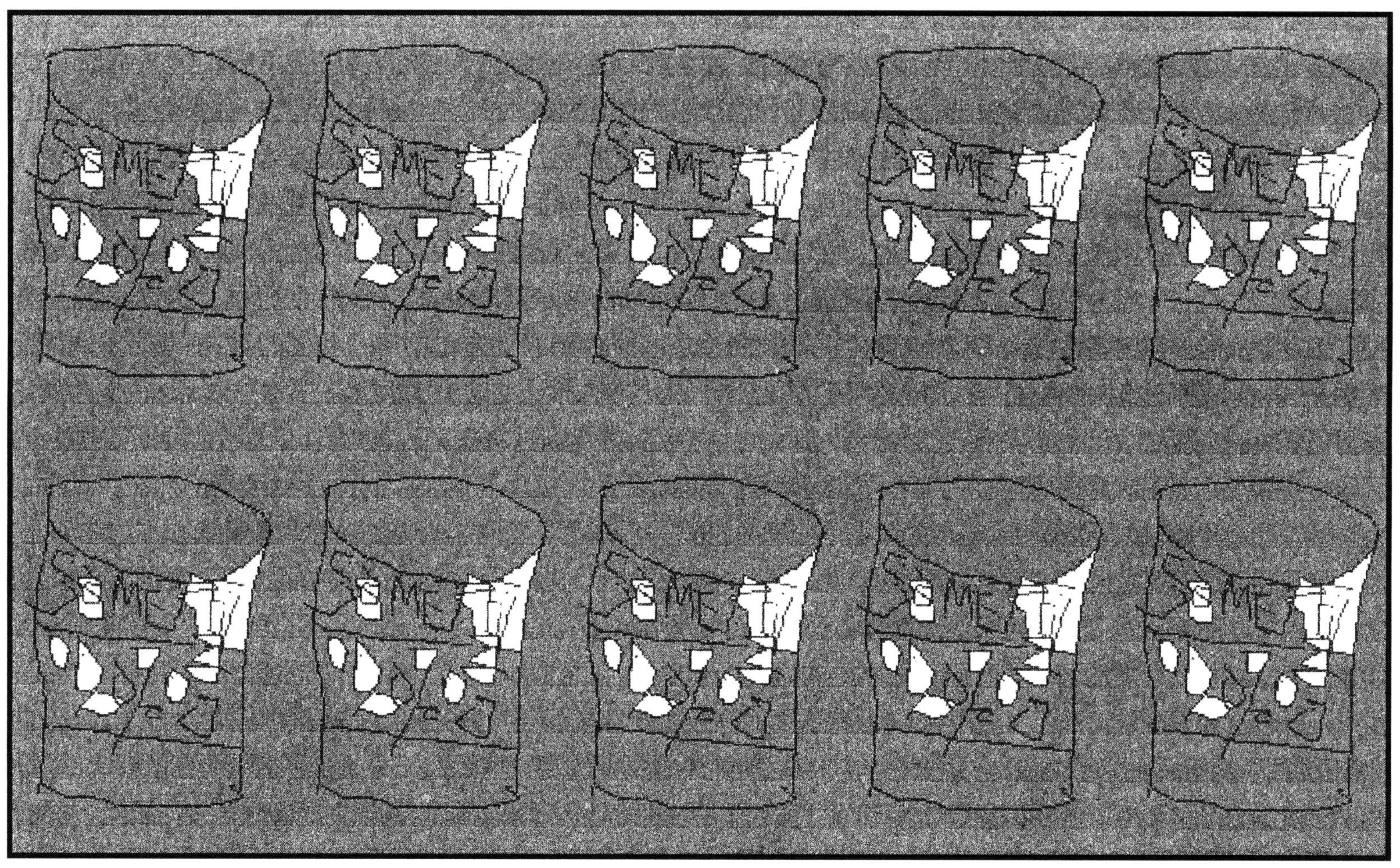

Jack Perham, Year 3 (image drawing using computer mouse and repeated)

Erasers and rulers

Rulers
For most drawing, children do not need rulers. Lines drawn with rulers tend to be similar so the resulting drawings are often without life and character. If pupils become dependent on rulers, they miss the opportunity to develop their ability to draw straight lines.

Erasers
Erasers create far worse problems. Although erasers may be used when areas of dark charcoal need to be lifted, to help create contrast and depth, the rest of the time they create more problems than they solve.

If children have used erasers in previous art classes, there are usually cries of indignation when their use is banned. Tell them that erasers destroy the surface of the paper, and further drawing on that surface is not as effective. Repeated rubbings out tend to crease the paper and look messy; heavy lines never rub out cleanly and always leave a grubby patch.

Some children may rub out almost everything they do and end up with little to show for their efforts.

Most important of all is the fact that, if children think they can rub something out, they tend not to approach the task with as much thought and observation as they should. They are more likely to launch into the drawing without those few extra moments of close looking and intense observation. They are inclined also, to place the drawing on the paper without much forethought, secure in the knowledge that they can rub it out.

Whilst enthusiasm and a desire to get started are wonderful, they must be weighed up against the value of deep thought and close looking. A good balance of both is ideal.

If they cannot use an eraser, they will need to be that bit more thoughtful and observant, and this is what will help them to progress.

Explain all this to them as it helps if they understand that the ban on erasers is better for their own artistic development.

Year 4 child's scraper drawing (see page 38)

Line

Year 4 child's doodle

Year 4 child's continuous line drawing

Rationale

Children's exploration of different lines in different media will enable them to use a range of lines in their own work. These activities will open their eyes to the huge variety of lines that they can use.

Children learning to draw lines soon discover that they are gaining control over a most powerful tool.

The simplest line suggests direction, divides space, and has length, width, tone and texture. It can enclose or define shape, and can suggest contour. It is with line that we create writing.

There are no limits to the possibilities of pencil. It is the most basic tool in the art of drawing and also one of the most versatile.

'Study for the Sfortza Monument' by Leonardo da Vinci, showing use of light lines (a larger, photocopiable version appears on page 129). Reproduced with permission from Windsor Castle

Drawing light lines

This is one of the areas that creates the most problems for children in drawing. The business of starting a drawing using light lines, so that you can alter them if necessary, is a very difficult one for children to grasp. This is not so vital in narrative drawing, but it becomes increasingly more important as children try to achieve a particular result.

Explaining to children why light lines are important

- ❒ Explain that when artists start out on a drawing they don't expect for one minute that they will get everything right first time. So they use light lines or marks that they can alter later if they need to.
- ❒ Children could be told: *'You have to start a drawing somewhere and you can't be sure you won't have to change something, so make it easier for yourself: start off with* **light** *lines. You can then put in the lines you think are better over the light lines.'*
- ❒ Show the children some examples of drawings by artists that show lines which have been drawn over, or next to, other lines. Drawings by Leonardo da Vinci are an excellent example. See Resource sheet 1 (page 129). Tell the children that he was a genius who worked as an artist for a very long time. He changed his drawings as he went along. The children will almost certainly want to change something too, so they should avoid using dark lines as it is much harder to change them.
- ❒ Say, for example, *'Leonardo didn't throw down his pencil when his drawings went wrong, saying, "I give up, I'm rubbish at drawing."'* Try to take the pressure off them to feel they must get it right first time.

Different ways to help children use light lines
Try inviting someone who can draw (it doesn't have to be an artist) to draw in front of the children, thinking out loud as the drawing progresses, altering things as they go along. It's better if the person isn't too accomplished, as making the children feel daunted would be counterproductive.

It helps if children understand that it is the amount of pressure on the pencil that results in the darkness of the line. Try asking them to close their eyes, make a line on the paper and then guess how dark it will be. Then ask them to make three more lines, each darker than the first, then three lighter ones. Look to see how well they have judged the darkness and lightness of the lines.

You could try referring to light lines as whispering or secret lines.

I talked to one newly qualified teacher whose class had produced some stunning drawings; you could clearly see light lines beneath the final ones. When I asked her how she had achieved this, she replied, *'Easy, I just gave them 2H pencils for the initial drawings, then 2B to improve and complete them.'* Then she added, *'If they do dark lines to begin with, I just tear the drawings up!'* Her first idea is worth a try.

About this chapter

Children's exploration of different lines in different media will enable them to use a range of lines in their own work. These activities will open their eyes to the huge variety of lines that they can use.

In this chapter children make their own line collections for future reference. They use the skill in a context. They experiment in a range of media, and investigate the use of line by other artists.

If you are short of time, do only the key skill lessons.

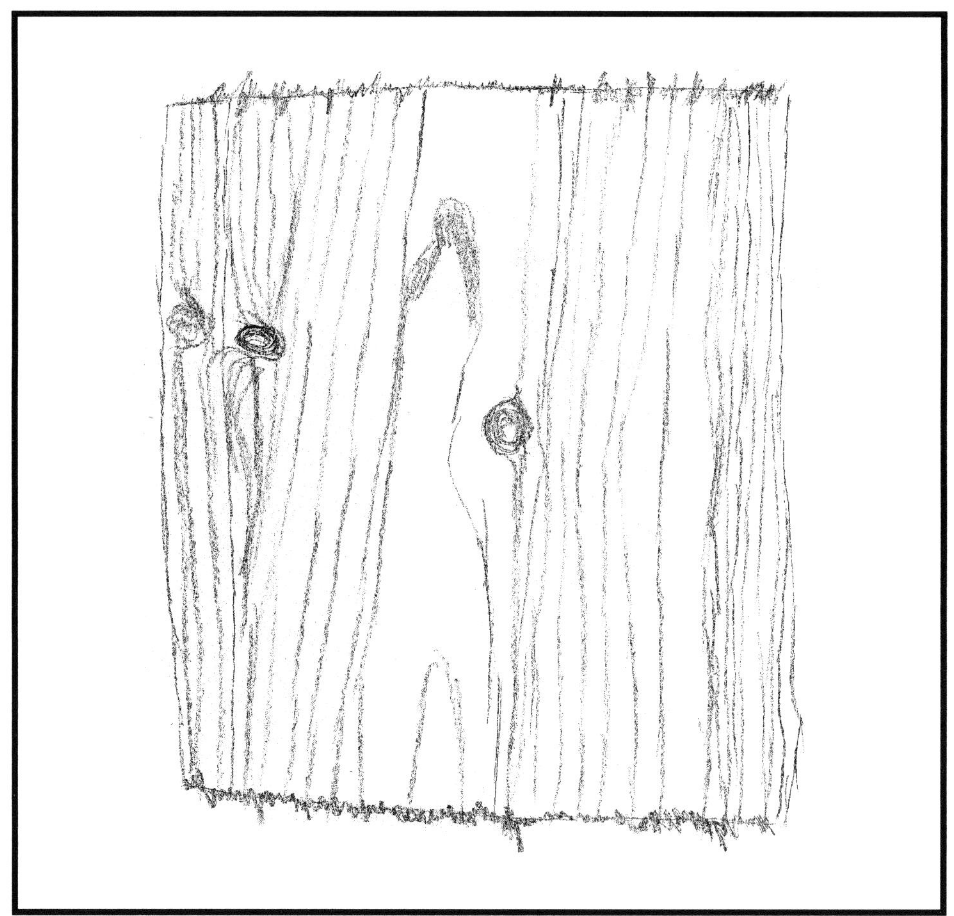

Jack Perham, Year 4 (pencil drawing of a piece of wood)

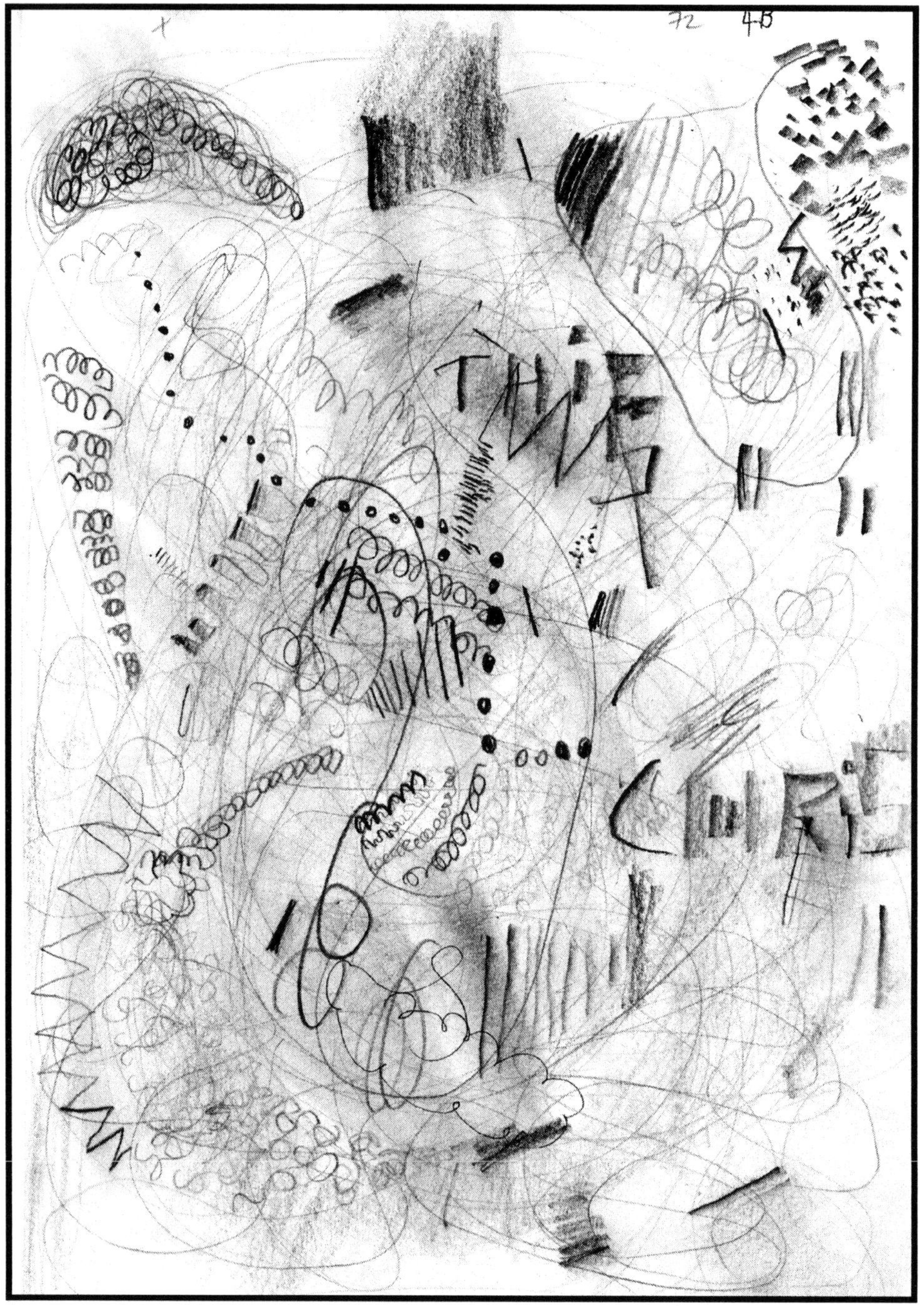

Year 3 child's collection of different lines in pencil

Making different types of lines in pencil

Time	Resources	National Curriculum
30 min.	B and 4B pencils Sketchbooks 1 set of drawing pencils H to 8B (if you have them) Large piece of white paper for teacher's modelling	2a, 4a

Introduction

'One way to improve your drawings and make them more interesting is to use lots of different kinds of lines. It is amazing how many different kinds of lines there are. You are going to make collections of lines in your sketchbooks. You will be able to look back at them when you are about to draw, to remind yourself of how many there are to use. It's a bit like using lots of interesting words to bring your writing to life. Using lots of different types of lines can bring your drawings to life.'

Practical activity

Teacher

- ❒ Show the set of drawing pencils and demonstrate the different grades.
- ❒ Explain that H stands for hard and B for black. The more Bs, the blacker the lead.
- ❒ Say they will be using the B and 4B today.

Children

Model each type of line you ask them to make.

- ❐ Using the 4B pencil the children make:
  - ✳ a short straight dark line
  - ✳ a short straight medium tone line
  - ✳ a short straight light line
  - ✳ a short straight nearly invisible line
  - ✳ a short straight line using the side of the lead (to use the side of the lead, the pencil should be held slightly differently, so the lead is as parallel to the paper as possible).
- ❐ Then the same five step sequence for:
  - ✳ a long straight line
  - ✳ short and long curved lines
  - ✳ long and short wavy lines, ziz-zags, and jagged lines
  - ✳ broken lines, dashes, dots
  - ✳ any other kinds of lines the children suggest.

Repeat with B pencils if there is time. Label line collections B or 4B.

This activity can be recorded in a formal (as shown on this page) or informal way (as shown on the previous page). However it is recorded, it must be done in such a way that it can easily be referred back to later.

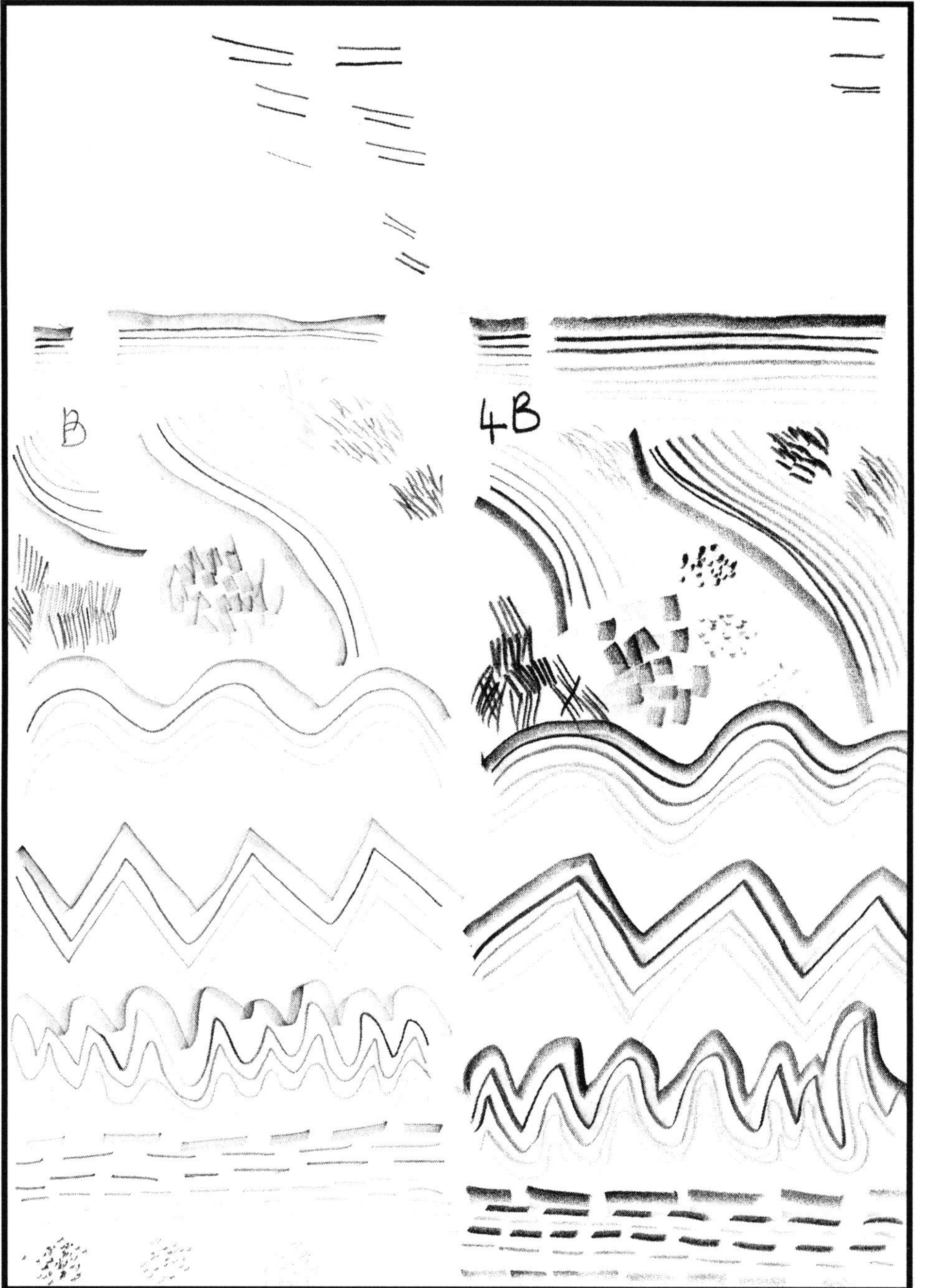

Year 4 child's example of making different lines in pencil

Different lines in pencil

Time	Resources	National Curriculum
30 min.	B and 4B pencils Sketchbooks If drawing cannot be done outside then use: pieces of wood with grain showing, leaves, flowers, seed heads, soft toys, clothes or topic artefacts (see list on page 69)	1a, 1c, 2b, 4a

As soon as possible after completing the line investigations (on pages 20–21), children should be given the opportunity to use a range of lines in a drawing. Teach that if they are drawing a subject that has hair or fur, they should draw lines that follow the form (three-dimensional shape). If the lines curve round the form, their drawings will look as if they have some depth and solidness.

Try to choose subject matter that gives the children scope to try out the skill: a model wearing stripes, an outdoor scene, school field or wild area that has grass and trees. They can even draw each other.

Introduction

'Now you are going to draw (whatever). *Try to use some of those lines you drew in your sketchbooks. Remember that lines can be light or dark, delicate or strong. You can use both the side and the point of the pencil and you can use whichever pencils that you think will do the job best.'*

Suggest that the children look back at their line collections occasionally while they are drawing.

Page 23 can be photocoped and used as an assessment activity. Before asking the children to draw a picture in the empty box, review the expectations with them.

Year 3 and 4 children's pencil drawings (face also appears on front cover)

Expectations after covering key skill

- ❒ All children will be able to draw a range of lines in two grades of pencil.
- ❒ Most will be able to use a number of these lines when drawing in context.
- ❒ A few children will be able to create different effects with different types of lines, appropriate to the subject.

Success criteria as explained to children

- ❒ You **must** include a variety of different lines in your drawing.
- ❒ You **should** use light and dark lines in places.
- ❒ You **could** use the side and point of your pencils.
- ❒ You **could** create special effects such as grass, prickles, fur, etc. (refer to the subject matter)

These criteria should really be drawn up with the pupils as the skill is being taught. Children can use the success criteria to make judgements about their work, followed by teacher judgements. For further information on success criteria see page 120.

Name ______________

Date ______________

'Haystacks near a Farm' by Vincent van Gogh (a larger, photocopiable version appears on page 130). Reproduced with permission from the Museum of Amsterdam

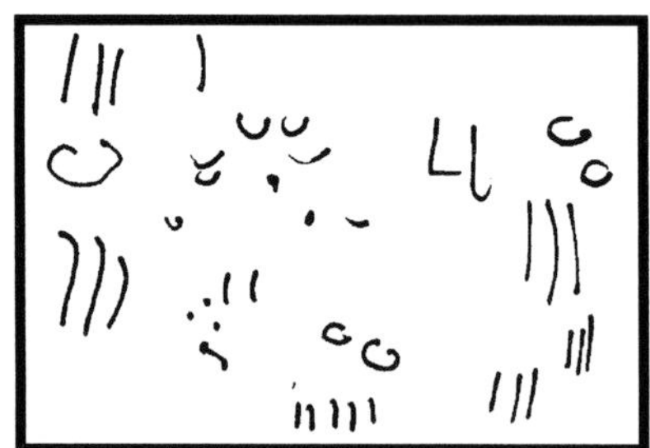

Examples of lines found by children using viewfinders

Looking at line in works of art 1

Time	Resources	National Curriculum
15 min.	Sketchbooks Viewfinders (see Glossary and page 74–75) B, 2B or 4B pencils Resource sheet 2 (page 130)	4a, 4c

Introduction

'You are going to look at a drawing done by Vincent van Gogh to see how many different kinds of lines have been used and how the artist has created different effects.'

Practical activity

❐ Give out at least one copy of Resource sheet 2 ('Haystacks near a Farm' by van Gogh) and one viewfinder between two children.
❐ Ask the children to slide the viewfinder over the picture and look at different parts of the picture.
❐ Ask them to choose an area to look at closely.
❐ Keeping the viewfinder in that one area, they look closely at the different types of lines inside the frame.
❐ Children copy these lines into their sketchbooks.
❐ This can be repeated with other areas of the picture.

Looking at line in works of art 2

Questioning with a line focus

Time	Resources	National Curriculum
15 min.	Resource sheet 3 (page 131)	3a, 4a, 4c, 5d

Introduction

'When you have had a good look at the picture and talked about it with the person next to you, I am going to ask you some questions about it.'

Activity

Give each pair of children a copy of 'Monnow Bridge' by John Sell Cotman (Resource sheet 3). Write the questions up on the board, or have a photocopy of them for the children to read as they look at the picture. This will help to focus their looking.

Questions

- ❒ What medium do you think the artist has used?
- ❒ What different kinds of lines have been used for the roofs? Describe them.
- ❒ How many different roof patterns can you see?
- ❒ How has the artist created darker areas such as shadows?
- ❒ Are all the lines the same thickness, darkness, length?
- ❒ If you had done this drawing, is there anything you would have changed? Why? How?

'Monnow Bridge' by John Sell Cotman (a larger, photocopiable version appears on page 131). Reproduced with permission from Tate, London 2005

Year 4 child's drawing of a Mendhi hand

Pens

Working in pen helps children create confident drawings. There is no possibility of rubbing out, and little opportunity to change lines. After some thought, they just have to launch into the drawing, knowing that what they put down will have to stay.

Fine line pens are very useful for crisp, delicate or detailed drawings. 0.4 mm is probably the finest tip appropriate to this age group.

Medium tip pens range from the average felt tip up to about 0.8 mm.

Broad pens could be anything from 1.6 mm upwards. The round tip is more manageable for Years 3–4 than the chisel tip, as the children tend to forget which way to angle the point. Broad pens are excellent for large-scale or group work. They are also good for creating borders for large-scale pictures.

Lovely effects can be achieved by wetting water-based pen drawings with a damp fine brush. The black line goes a soft dark brown or grey green, and the lines blur a little. If the tip of a wet brush is touched against the lines, the ink can be spread across a small area. This is known as bleeding or moving.

Permanent pens are extremely useful as paint or inks can be added to the drawings without the ink running. It is difficult to buy permanent fine pens, so the drawings can be photocopied and then paint added. Berol® make a double-ended permanent pen which has tips of two different thicknesses.

Thomas Ellis, Year 4

Making different lines with fine, medium and broad line pens

Time	Resources	National Curriculum
15 min.	Fine line pens (approx. 0.4 mm tip) Medium tip pens (approx. 0.8 mm tip) Broad round tip pens (approx. 1.6 mm tip) Sketchbooks	2b, 4a

Introduction

'Pens have tips of different sizes and it depends on what you are drawing as to which pen you need to use. You are going to try making different lines with different pens.'

Practical activity

- ❒ Put a few pens of all the different sizes on their tables.
- ❒ Children then draw lines with each of the three pens:
  - ✳ a short straight line
  - ✳ a long straight line
  - ✳ a short and long curved line
  - ✳ a long and short wavy line
  - ✳ a ziz-zag and a jagged line
  - ✳ broken lines, dashes, dots
  - ✳ any other kinds of lines the children suggest.
- ❒ You could ask them which pens they think would be best for drawing, for example, a piece of lace, a packed lunch or a building.

Jack Perham, Year 4

Drawing with fine, medium and broad line pens

Time	Resources	National Curriculum
45 min. approx.	Fine, medium and broad pens Sketchbooks	1a, 2a, 4a

Introduction

'You have experimented making lines with three different types of pen. In the next drawing you can try using all three pens in the same picture.'

Practical activity

❒ Put a selection of pens out on each table.
❒ Children select an aspect of the classroom to draw.
❒ Ask them to decide what things would be best drawn in which pen.
❒ Point out that in this room there are some things you might want to draw in fine pens, some in medium pens and some in broad pens.
❒ Point out different main features in the room – doors, windows, – which could be drawn in broad pens.
❒ Ask which items could be drawn using medium pens.
❒ Draw their attention to small detail, like light switches and fittings, sockets, skirting boards. Encourage them to include people and equipment.
❒ The length of the lesson will depend on the detail included.

Year 3 drawing using two sizes of pen

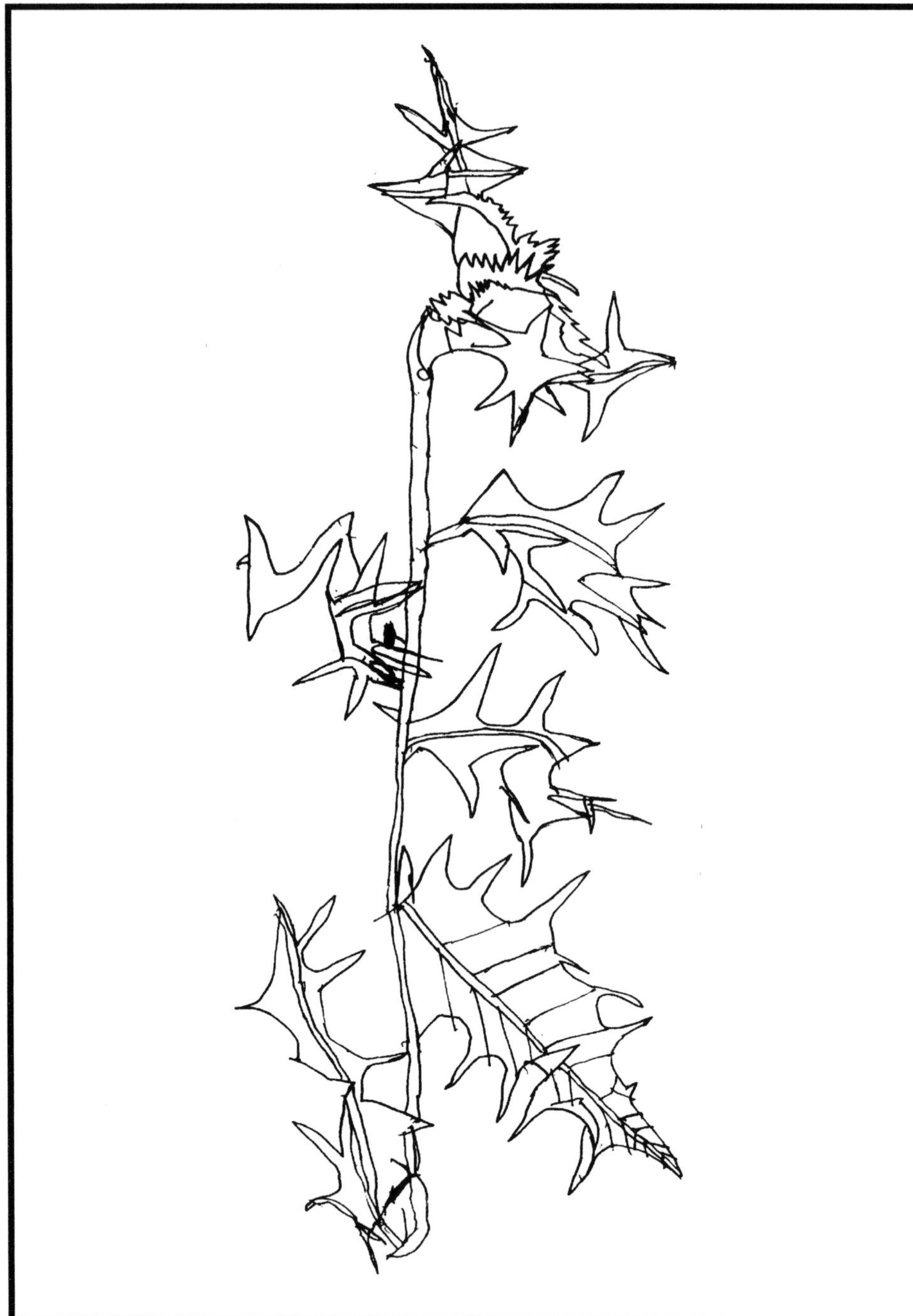

Hugh White, Year 4

USING SKILL Fine line pens

Time	Resources	National Curriculum
30 min.	Fine line pens (0.4 mm tip) Sketchbooks Small-scale artefacts with intricate detail such as: leaves, flowers, feathers, shells, lace, etc. or topic artefacts (see list on page 69) Magnifying glasses	1a, 2a, 4a

Introduction

'Fine line pens are excellent for drawing small, delicate or detailed objects. Don't use them for solid colouring in, as that would wear out the fine tips.'

Practical activity

- ❐ Ask children to look carefully at the shapes, patterns and textures they can see before they start to draw.
- ❐ Ask them to discuss what they can see with a partner.
- ❐ They should use the magnifying glasses if they need to.
- ❐ Ask them to think about how they will place the drawing on the paper before they start to draw.
- ❐ Tell them to put in as much detail as they can.

Medium line pens

Time	Resources	National Curriculum
20 min.	Medium pens Sketchbooks Collection of suitable artefacts (can be topic-related or could be from around the classroom) – see list on page 69	1a, 2a, 4a

Introduction

'Medium tip pens make a good strong line. They are very useful when you are drawing quickly. They will allow you to do some detail, but not as much as a fine line pen.'

Practical activity

- ❒ Ask the children to suggest objects they think would look good drawn with a medium pen. Guide their choices.
- ❒ Tell the children:
  - ✳ Some aspects of the subject may be masked by other parts
  - ✳ Take a good look before you start as you will not be able to change anything
  - ✳ Consider how you will place the drawing on the paper before starting the drawing.

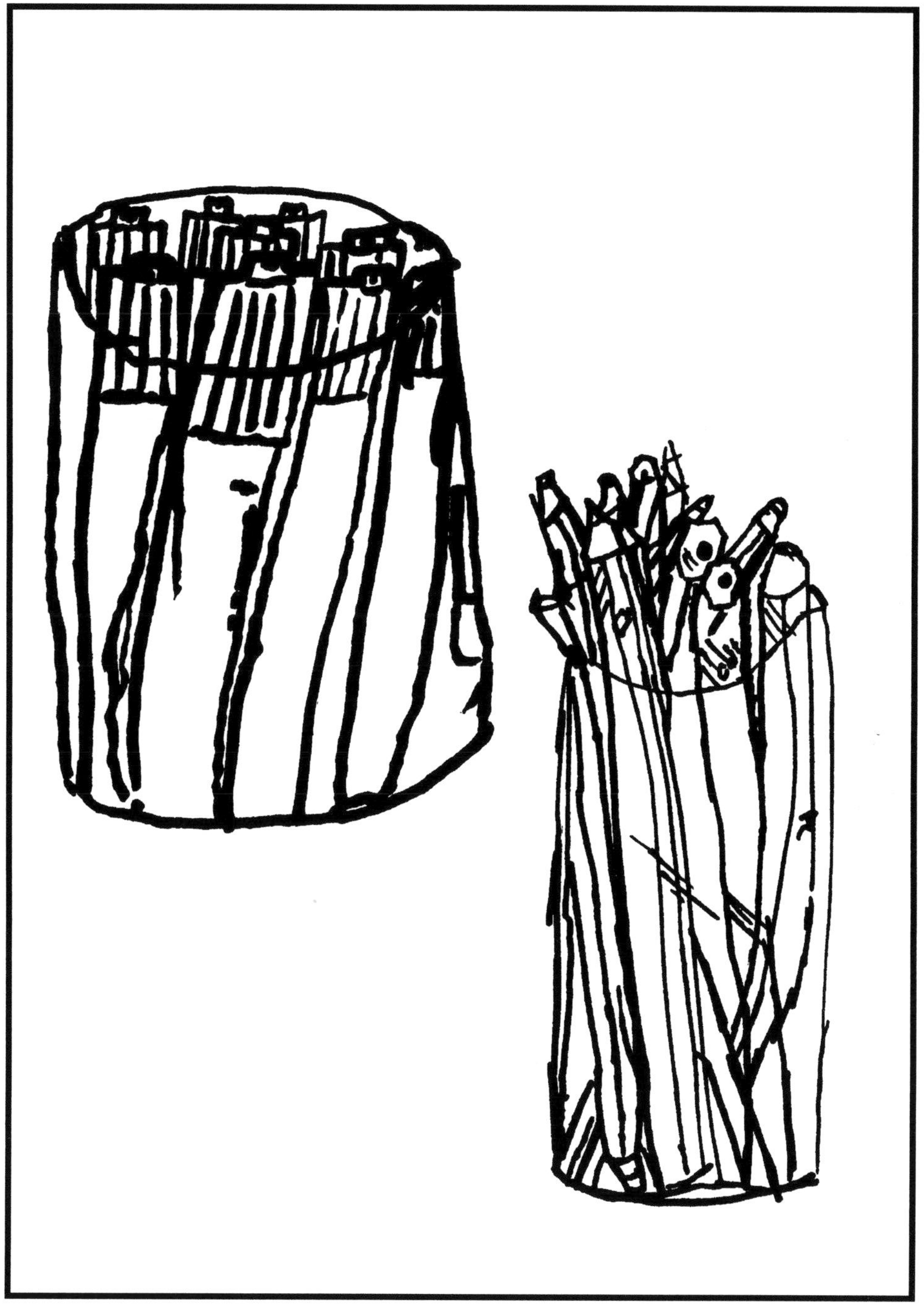

Year 3 children's pen drawings

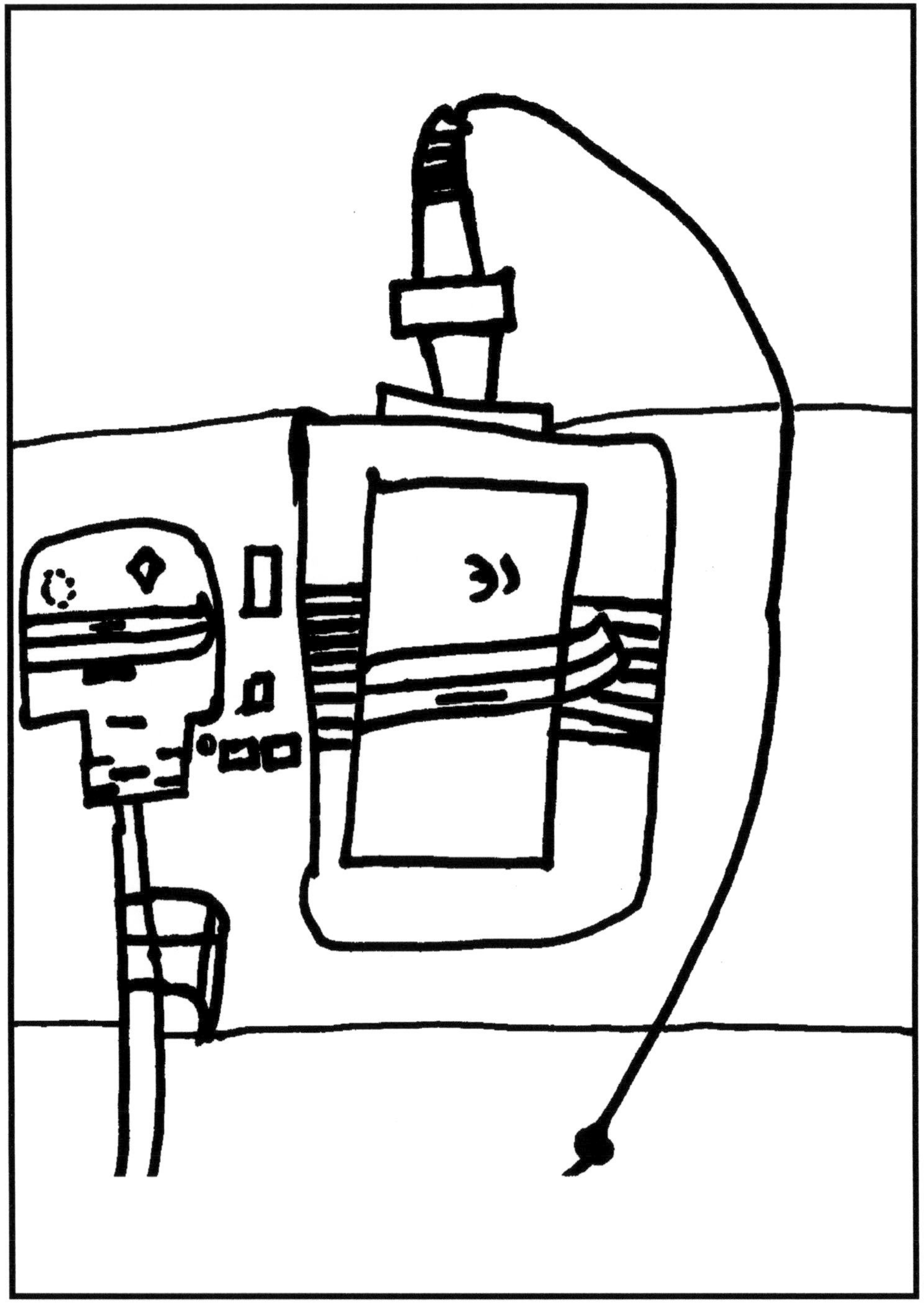

Oliver Coulham, Year 4 (drawing of electric plugs in broad pen)

Broad line pens

Time	Resources	National Curriculum
20 min.	Broad pens, round tip if possible (use permanent pens if colour washes are to be added over the top) Sketchbooks	1a, 2a, 4a

Warning!

Permanent pens go through the paper onto the next page in the sketchbook, or onto the table if you are working on paper. Put newspaper underneath.

Introduction

'Broad pens are brilliant when you want to do large or dramatic drawings. Today you will be drawing (whatever) *and we are aiming for a bold, clear drawing without much detail. Look for the main shapes.'*

Practical activity

- ❒ Ask the children to choose something in the room that they think would look good drawn with a broad pen.
- ❒ Guide their choices. Classroom furniture is a good option.
- ❒ If chisel tip pens are being used, suggest they use both sides of the tip.
- ❒ When drawings are completed, ask them if they think they could have drawn the subject as well with a fine or medium pen.

Background information

Broad pens are excellent for group work. The round tip pens are more manageable than the chisel tips, although less versatile. If permanent pens have been used, colour washes could be applied over the drawings.

Playing around with line

Time	Resources	National Curriculum
45 min. approx.	Fine line pens Sketchbooks or A4 paper Enlarged copy of Resource sheet 4 (page 132)	4a, 5d

Introduction

'Line can be used in many ways; you can use it to play tricks on the eye, to create the illusion of movement. This is what you are going to do today.'

Practical activity

❒ Show the example of Op Art on Resource sheet 4.

❒ Talk about how the artist has used lines to give the illusion of movement.

❒ Ask the children to draw four or five geometrical shapes – diamonds, squares, etc. – dotted about the page.

❒ Ask them to draw decreasing shapes inside the original shape.

❒ Now they draw lines that travel across the page which alter direction as they go round shapes.

❒ Tell them to draw each subsequent line so that it follows the last closely, but not touching – rather like water flowing round boulders in a stream.

❒ Stress that they should draw the lines as carefully and as close together as they can.

Background information
Explain that Bridget Riley is a meticulous artist who uses lines, shapes and colours with precision to create particular effects. Her drawings and paintings deliberately give the illusion of movement. She is a British artist with an international reputation.

Billie Reay, Year 3 (drawing in fine line pen, giving the illusion of movement)

Cross-hatching 1

Using line to create tone

Time	Resources	National Curriculum
30 min.	Sketchbooks Fine line pens B and 4B pencils Resource sheet 5 (page 133)	2a, 4a

Introduction

'When line is used to create tone it is known as shading. If the shading is made with single lines it is called single-hatching and if the lines cross each other it is called cross-hatching.'

Practical activity

- ❒ Show some examples of hatching on Resource sheet 5.
- ❒ Create some kind of framework for recording the cross-hatching. A series of boxes is fine, or children might like to devise their own.
- ❒ Start with the fine line pen. Draw diagonal lines close together, then some crossing the other way. In the next box do the same but have the lines a little further apart. Aim to create three or four tones in each media.

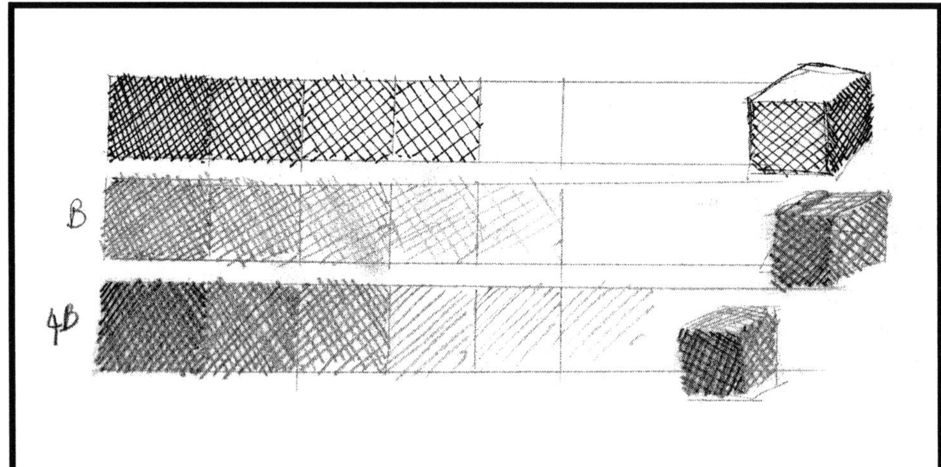

Year 4 child's recording of cross-hatching in pencil

- ❒ Do the same with a B pencil, but you can also introduce the idea that the lines can become slightly lighter with each box, as well as further apart.
- ❒ Repeat with 4B pencil.
- ❒ While they are doing this, draw a cube for each child (it's better to do it for them, as they will get bogged down trying to draw cubes, and the focus of the lesson will become confused).

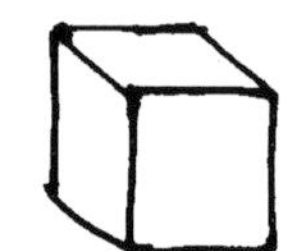

- ❒ Using one of the media, children shade one side of the cube a dark degree of cross-hatching, one side a medium degree and one side a light. They should then be able to see how shading can create the illusion of three dimensions.

Background information

It will help children to see the different depths and types of tone possible in cross-hatching if they experiment in different drawing media.

One way of introducing this is to show some clear examples. The illustrator Edward Ardizzone, whose illustrations some of the children may know from *Stig of the Dump*, uses cross-hatching a great deal.

Cross-hatching 2

Time	Resources	National Curriculum
30 min.	Sketchbooks Fine line pens or B or 4B pencils View of some buildings (if this is not possible work from a photograph – estate agents' pictures are quite useful)	1a, 4a

Introduction

'Now you have tried out different kinds of cross-hatching, see if you can use that technique to create the illusion of solid forms in your next drawing.'

Practical activity

- ❒ Ask the children to look at the view or the photograph (see Resources box, above).
- ❒ They decide first which are the darkest tones, then the medium tones, and then the lightest.
- ❒ They can discuss this with a partner.
- ❒ Remind them how they can achieve the effect of different tones with cross-hatching.
- ❒ They could refer back to the relevant page in their sketchbooks from the previous lesson.
- ❒ Ask them to draw the outline of the buildings first and then create the tones using cross-hatching.
- ❒ Ask them to consider whether they have created a more three-dimensional effect than they would have achieved with just a line drawing.
- ❒ They could consider creating different tones in the background using single hatching.

Year 3 child's pen drawing using cross-hatching

Year 4 child's pen drawing using cross-hatching

Making different lines in charcoal

Time	Resources	National Curriculum
15 min.	Charcoal, broken into short lengths Sketchbooks Fixative (see Glossary) Protection for clothing	2a, 4a

There is information about charcoal in the chapter on Chalk and charcoal, pages 112–113.

Introduction

'Charcoal is the oldest drawing material known to man. It is made of specially burned wood and as it is very brittle it will break easily. It makes wonderful dark lines, but it can be used lightly too. One of its special qualities is that it smudges, but today you are only concerned with the different lines you can make with it.'

Practical activity

❐ Children should cover clothes and push back sleeves.

❐ Ask the children to try out all the different types of lines they can with the charcoal:

- ✱ long, short
- ✱ light, medium, dark
- ✱ straight, curved, wavy
- ✱ broken
- ✱ dots, dashes.

❐ Remind children to experiment using the side of the charcoal.

❐ Spray the work with fixative when pupils are out of the room.

Jack Perham, Year 3

Drawing with charcoal

Time	Resources	National Curriclum
Figures: 1 min each Scenes: 20 min.	Charcoal Sketchbooks Fixative (see Glossary)	1a, 2a, 4a

Introduction

'Now you have tried making different lines in charcoal, you are going to do some drawings using whichever of those lines you think will be best. You may want to use lots of different lines, or all of one kind – it will depend on what you are drawing.'

Practical activities

Figure drawing

- ❐ Ask a child to pose for one minute only. Aim for an action pose.
- ❐ The rest of the class draw the pose as quickly as they can, trying to capture a feeling of movement.
- ❐ Repeat with several different poses.

Outdoor scene

- ❐ Select a view outside where there is plenty of scope to draw foliage.
- ❐ Remind the children to work fast and use lots of different lines to create different effects.

Background information
Charcoal is excellent for helping children to draw quickly and freely. This lesson encourages that. Charcoal photocopies well and photocopied drawings can look very good with watercolour added later.

Photocopy of Year 4 child's charcoal drawing of a one minute action pose

Scraper technique

Time:	Resources	National Curricululm
1 hour	Cartridge paper (see Glossary) Coloured crayons Oil pastels (optional) Cocktail sticks or paper clips (as scrapers) Tissue or rags for polishing Enlarged copy of Resoure sheet 6 (page 134)	2a

Introduction

'You are going to create some line drawings today using a different method. It is called the scraper technique, and it makes some interesting and unusual effects.'

Practical activity

Show the children the example of children's work illustrated opposite and also Paul Klee's drawing (Resource sheet 6). Explain the technique to the children.

Technique

- ❒ Cover the paper with a good layer of crayon. This can be single or multicoloured, depending on what effect you want to achieve.
- ❒ Next cover this with a thick solid layer of a dark crayon or oil pastel. (Oil pastels are softer and the layer is slightly easier to apply than with crayon.)
- ❒ Polish this layer of dark crayon to create a smooth surface.
- ❒ The picture or design is then scraped off using cocktail sticks to reveal the colours beneath.
- ❒ It might help them to get the feel of how it works if they do a very small test piece first. This could then be stuck in sketchbooks, and annotated.
- ❒ Partly unwound paper clips make good scrapers.

Year 3 child's scraper drawing of a pirate battle

Background information

Scraper work is really first cousin to printing, having links with etching. However, as primary children are most unlikely to have experience of etching, it fits quite well here in the Line chapter. Paul Klee's drawings are a good stimulus. They are not created using the scraper technique but they look as if they could be. Scraper work enables the children to see line in a different colour context. It gives line a new dimension. Children need to have roughly planned their designs before scraping off the top layer. If there is no natural link to another subject area, night-time or underwater scenes can look great, or even just doodle patterns.

Jordan Clark, Year 4

Tone

James Chapman, Year 4

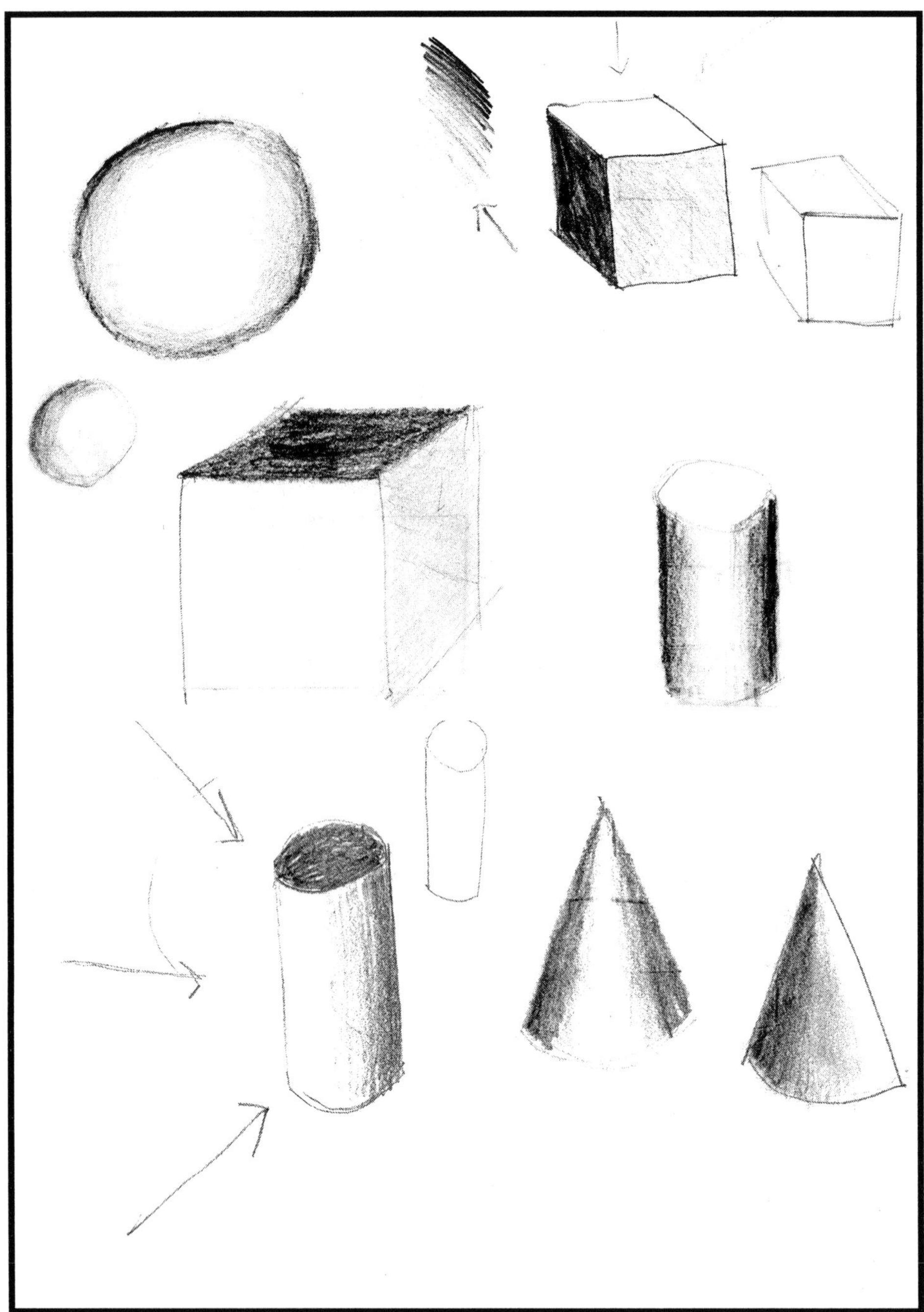

Year 4 child's shading of 3-D geometrical shapes in pencil

Rationale

The lightness or darkness of a colour, such as the shades of grey in the gradual change from black to white, is called tone.

Children can use tone to create the illusion of form and solidity, to create mood or to direct the viewer's attention.

Tone can make the whole effect of a drawing more dramatic and interesting.

The gradual transition of tone from light to dark was once regarded as essential to good drawing.

'Light and shadows should blend without line or borders in the manner of smoke.'
Leonardo da Vinci,
Treatise on Painting

About this chapter

Children can use tone to create the illusion of form and space.

In this chapter they will learn how to make different tones in soft pencil and charcoal.

They will try to create the illusion of form and weight using different tones in pencil and charcoal.

They will then use this skill in a context.

The ability to shade meaningfully with a pencil is perhaps one of the most elusive aspects of drawing.

If you only have time for one skill, do the key skill.

Completed charcoal tone sheet (see page 136)

Making different tones in pencil

Time	Resources	National Curriculum
25 min.	Sketchbooks HB, B, 2B and 4B pencils, or as wide a range as you can collect Large piece of white paper for teacher modelling Enlarged copy of Resource sheet 7 (page 135) Resource sheet 8 (page 136)	1c, 2b, 4a

Introduction

'If you look at these two drawings (show Resource sheet 7) *you will notice that one is a line drawing and the other uses line and tone. Using tone in your drawings as well as line will help your drawings look as if the subject matter has shape and weight, it will give the illusion of solidness. Today you are going to try out all the different tones you can make in HB, B, 2B and 4B pencils.'*

Practical activity

- ❒ Put a selection of pencils on each table.
- ❒ Model some of the different tones that can be made with the different pencils.
- ❒ Explain that the darkness or lightness of tone is created by increasing or decreasing the pressure.
- ❒ Children try them for themselves, starting with the darkest tone and gradually getting lighter.
- ❒ Explain that using the side of the pencil lead will create wider areas of tone.
- ❒ Children experiment with the range of tones possible with the full range of pencils HB to 4B.
- ❒ Label them.
- ❒ Children could try creating soft tones by smuding pencil marks.
- ❒ They could decide how to record these, or you could use the record sheet on Resource sheet 8.

A Year 3 child's experiments with making different tones in pencil

Using different tones in pencil

Time	Resources	National Curriuclum
25 min.	Sketchbooks 4B and B pencils	1c, 2b, 4a

Introduction

'Today you will be drawing a whole-body portrait. You should be trying to use tone to make the figure look solid rather than flat. Notice how the shadows curve round the body following the shape.'

Practical activity

- ❐ Select a model.
- ❐ Remind children to try to use as many tones as they can.
- ❐ Ask which is the darkest tone they can see on the model, and which is the lightest.
- ❐ Ask which of two mid tones is the lighter. For example, ask if the navy blue sweatshirt is darker/lighter than the grey trousers.
- ❐ Explain that colours have tones as well as shades. If they look at a black and white photograph, each colour will have a slightly different tone – yellow will be lighter than red, green could be lighter or darker than a blue.
- ❐ Suggest they narrow their eyes to try to judge darker or lighter areas on the model.
- ❐ Children could consider including tones in the background.
- ❐ Allow 15 minutes or so for the first drawing in one pencil, then change the model for the second pose and use the other grade of pencil.

Background information
Portraits are a good vehicle for encouraging children to use tone in drawings. For example, black shoes, dark grey trousers, mid-tone sweatshirt, varying skin tones, white collar. Choose the model carefully, preferably someone who is not wearing highly patterned clothes or the children may become sidetracked into drawing the patterns.

Year 3 child's pencil portrait. The dark background enhances the subtle tones on the figure

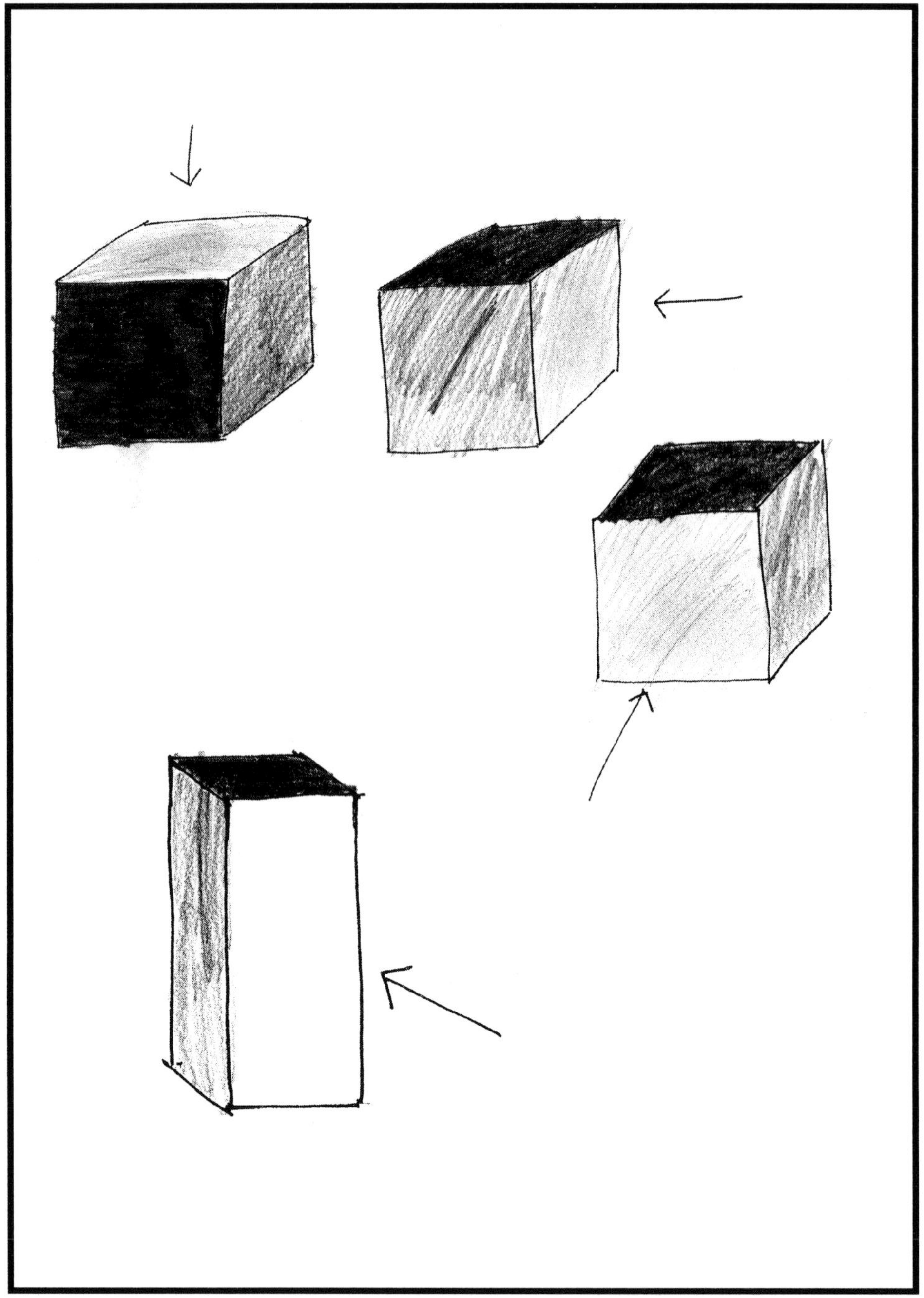

Jade Tanton, Year 4

Using tone to shade three-dimensional shapes

Time	Resources	National Curriculum
15 min.	4B pencils Three-dimensional mathematical shapes: a cube and a cylinder Sketchbooks or copies of Resource sheet 9 (page 137). If you are not using the worksheet you may need to draw 3 cubes, and 3 cylinders in their sketchbooks, as many children find this difficult.	1a, 4a

Introduction

'You have made different tones with B and 4B pencils. Now you are going to use those tones to try to make flat shapes look three-dimensional.'

Practical activity

Teacher

- ❒ Hold up the cube; discuss where the light falls, where the darkest and lightest tones are.
- ❒ Demonstrate how each surface of the cube is a different tone. If possible move the cube so that the light falls in different ways.
- ❒ Hold up the cylinder next. Draw attention to the way the tones change gradually around the surface of the cylinder.

Children

- ❒ Shade the surfaces of the drawn cube, one very dark, one medium and one light.
- ❒ Shade the surfaces of the other cubes with the tones in different positions.
- ❒ Ask them to think where the light is coming from in each case.
- ❒ Draw attention to the three-dimensional effect they have created.
- ❒ Explain that they could use tones like this when they are drawing buildings or solid shapes with corners.
- ❒ Before they shade the cylinders, ask children to decide if the light is coming from the left or right.

- Children now shade the darkest tone on the side furthest from the light (you may need to model this) using pencil strokes that run up and down the cylinder.
- Explain they must gradually lighten the tone as they shade in around the cylinder, leaving the side nearest to the light almost white. The top could be any tone depending on the direction of the light source.
- Point out that necks are cylinders. When they draw portraits they could look at how the light falls, and shade in a similar way.

Potential pitfall!

Children may find it difficult to shade gradually across the cylinders. If the tones change abruptly from dark to light, or the shading lines run across the cylinder rather than up and down the length, it will make the cylinder look stripy and flat rather than curved and three-dimensional. Revise gradual shading, as in the key skill lesson (page 42).

Spheres are even more tricky. Children will need to shade around the inside of the circle in a circular movement. Each concentric shading should be progressively lighter. The shading can be blended using the tips of the fingers.

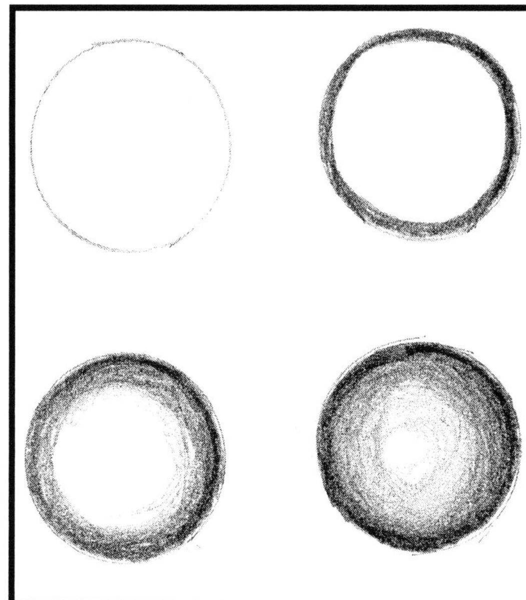

How to shape a sphere

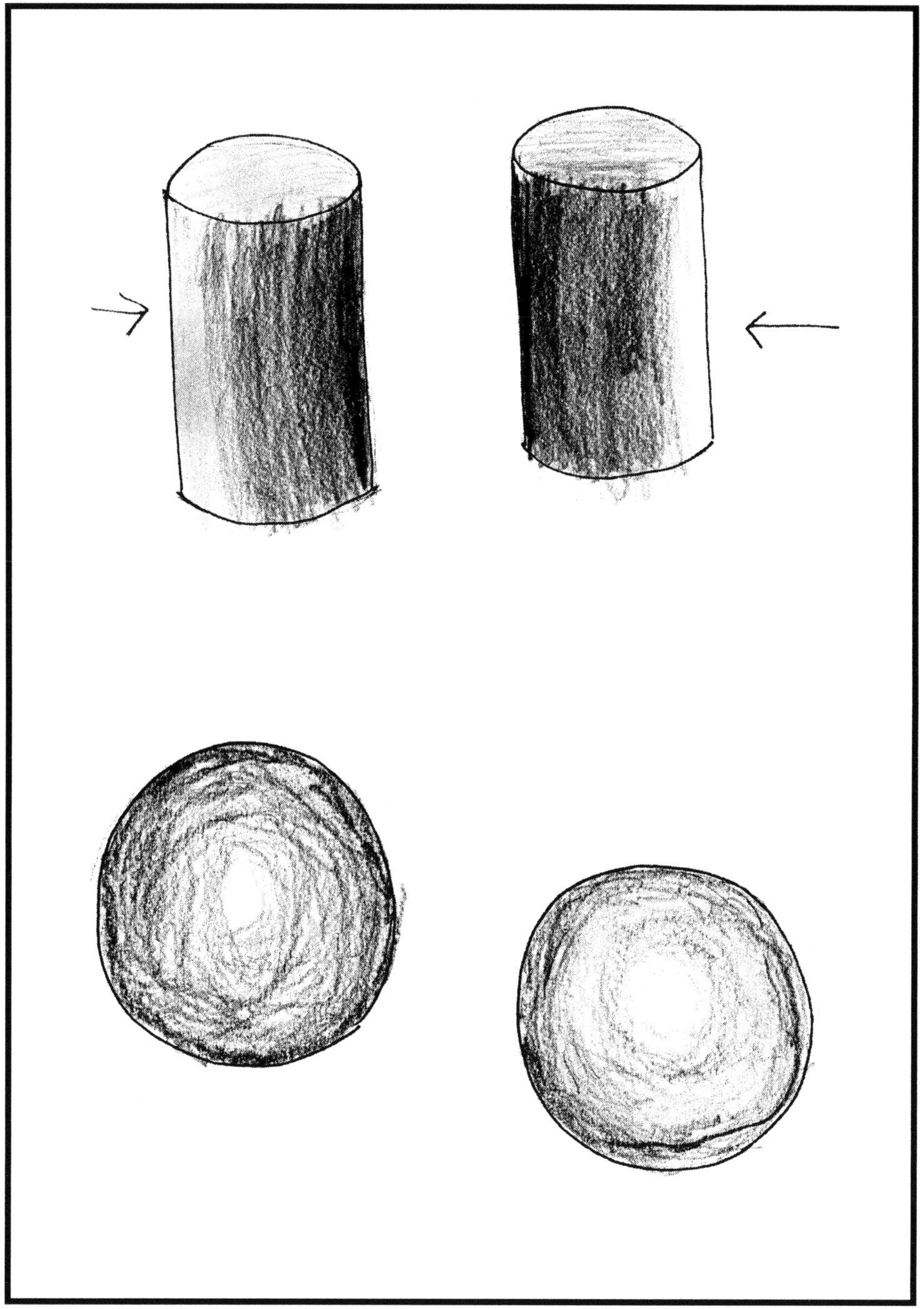

Jade Tanton, Year 4

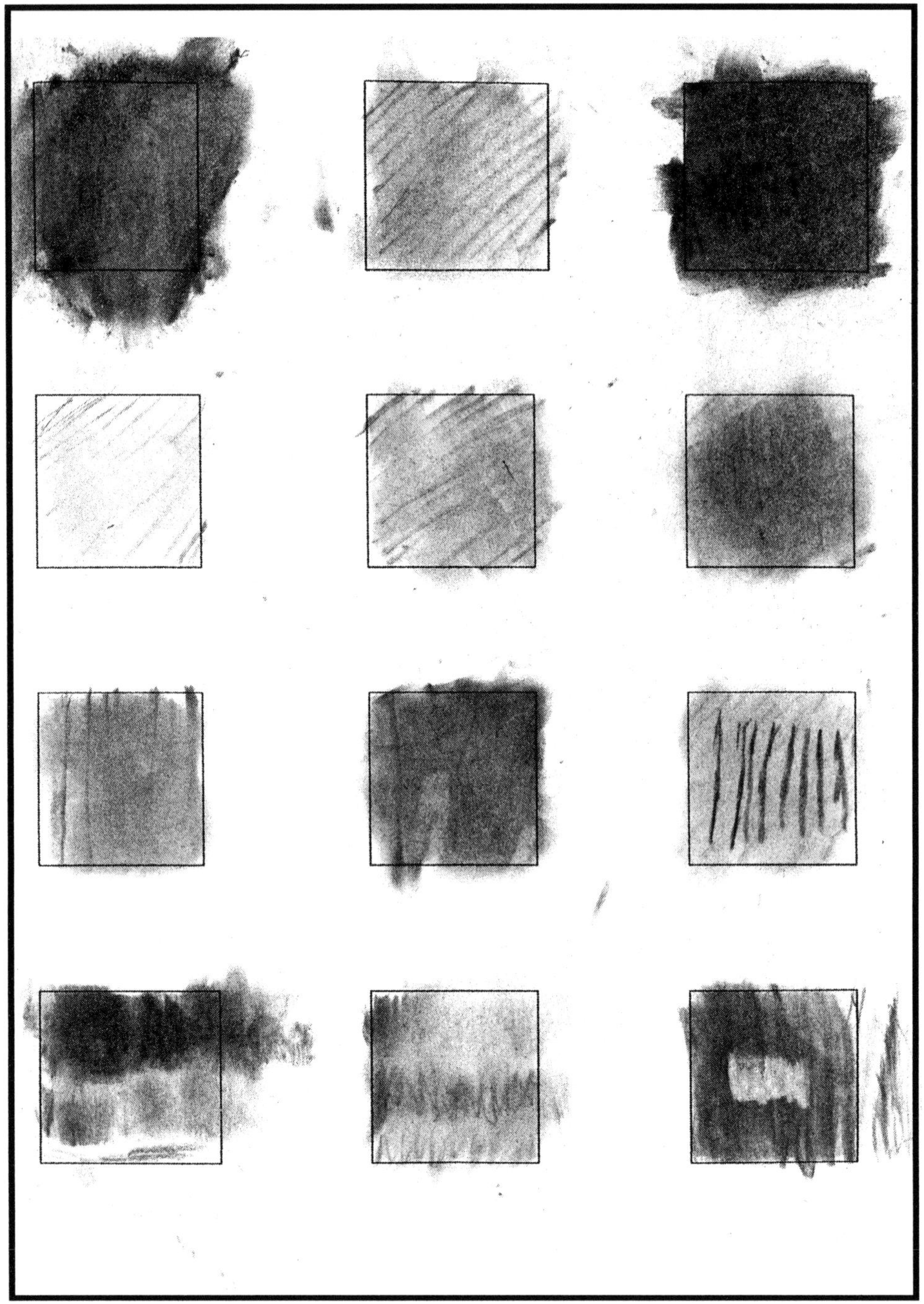

Raymond Penfold, Year 3 (see also example on page 41)

Making different tones with charcoal

Time	Resources	National Curricululm
15–20 min.	Sketchbooks Charcoal, medium thickness (broken into 4 cm lengths) Fixative (see Glossary) Resource sheet 8 (page 136) Scrap paper	2a, 2b, 4a

To make sure that drawings are not spoiled by being leaned on and smudged as work progresses, provide the children with a piece of scrap paper that can be laid over any completed sections of their work. Drawings can be sprayed with fixative at the end of the session, when children have left the room. Snap the charcoal into short lengths of about 4 cm – it won't break so readily and it will enable them to make marks using the side as well as the point of the charcoal.

Introduction

'Charcoal is made of burned wood and tends to break easily. It can make very dark marks or light marks depending on how hard you press. One of the main characteristics of charcoal is that it smudges easily and so you can make some really good smoky effects. It is very useful for quick sketching and for creating dramatic scences. Today you are going to investigate all the different tones you can make with charcoal.'

Practical activity

- ❒ Children make a series of marks that start very dark and gradually get lighter. This could be done on Resource sheet 8 as shown on this page, or in a more informal way, as shown on page 47.
- ❒ Suggest they try this first with the point of the charcoal and then the side, creating lines of different widths.
- ❒ Children then draw some marks close together and smudge them, blending the marks into areas of solid tone.
- ❒ Next experiment by creating tones of varying darkness.

- ❐ Draw a cube on their paper while they are doing this (see page 34). Ask the children to shade one side of the cube dark, one side medium and to leave one light.
- ❐ They could try drawing a circle and blending the tones with a finger around the edge, getting lighter towards the middle.
- ❐ Year 4 pupils could draw a cylinder and try spreading the tones around the sides of a cylinder. Help the less able to draw the ellipse.

Year 4 child's recording of different tones in charcoal

Year 4 child's drawing of a shoe using contrasting tones

Creating tone with charcoal

Time	Resources	National Curriculum
30 min.	Mid-tone sugar paper Charcoal, medium thickness (broken into 4 cm lengths) Fixative (see Glossary) Scrap paper to cover drawing as it progresses	1a, 2a, 2b, 4a, 5a

If the weather permits, take children outside to draw school buildings or trees as these will give plenty of scope for drawing strong shapes and shadows. If this is not possible then shoes, portraits or large houseplants are also good subjects. Try to ensure they don't get sidetracked into adding detail, patterns, etc.

Introduction

'Now you have experimented with the tones you can make with charcoal, you are going to draw (whatever)*, from looking especially carefully at the different tones.'*

Practical activity

- ❐ Get the children to do a quick, light line drawing, sketching in the main composition or framework of the subject.
- ❐ Now they should look for the darkest areas, and shade them in.
- ❐ Children could narrow their eyes to try to assess the main dark, medium and light tones they can see.
- ❐ They should leave the lightest areas unshaded, allowing the paper to show through.
- ❐ Lastly, create the various 'in between' tones by smudging, or by blending a series of marks.
- ❐ This is useful for foliage on trees, clouds, and skin tones.

Texture

Year 4 child's chalk drawing of pine spring

Year 4 child's pencil drawing of pine sprig

Definition

The following definition can be given to children: Texture is the word that explains how things feel when we touch them. In drawing it is the marks made on a surface which represent the way textures look.

Textural surfaces are experienced through both touch and sight.

Rationale

Texture can add interest and definition to a drawing. Children can use drawn texture to create the illusion of difference between one surface and another, for example fur and skin, grass and stone.

Children can use texture to give their drawings variety and interest, to differentiate between one area and another, and to make their drawings visually more exciting.

About this chapter

In this chapter children will record ways of representing textures, using different drawing media on different papers.

They will then use some of these techniques, drawing from first-hand observation.

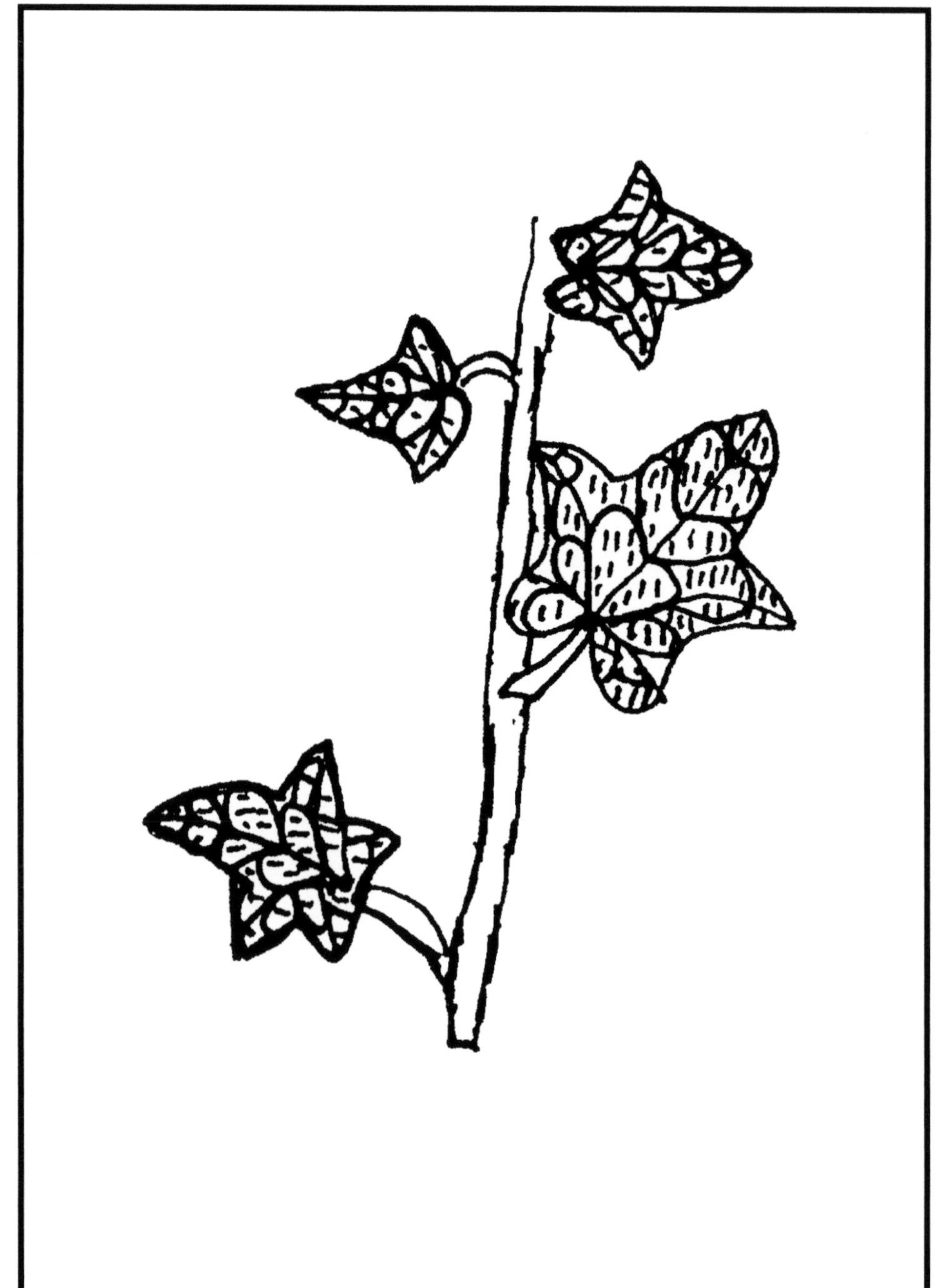

Year 3 child's pen drawing of ivy

Drawing different textures

Time	Resources	National Curriculum
30–40 min.	Sketchbooks Variety of drawing media: B or 2B pencils, felt tips, ball-point pens Collection of artefacts that have different textures: shells, orange peel, bark, fur, sacking or rough stone (see list on page 69) Large piece of white paper for teacher modelling	1a, 1c, 2a, 2b, 4a, 4b

Introduction

'You are going to be looking at, feeling and drawing different textures today. Texture is a word that explains how things feel when we touch them. You can see and feel textures. Texture is all around us, on ourselves … our skin, our hair and our clothes. In nature we see and feel it on bark, shells, animal skins and rough stone. Our eyes give information about the texture of things, but we can also feel them.'

Practical activity

- ❐ Ask children to feel the different textures of their skin, hair, desk, etc.
- ❐ Give a collection of textured objects to children. Allow a few minutes for them to feel the items and talk about them.
- ❐ Discuss some texture words the children can write in their sketchbooks: rough, smooth, prickly, coarse.
- ❐ Children make a series of marks to represent the texture of each artefact, labelling the artefact or the texture.
- ❐ Suggest trying different media.
- ❐ Point out that an artefact may have more than one texture.
- ❐ Model some marks, for example dots for sandpaper, little dashes for fur or scribbly lines for wool.

Background information

Texture is often introduced to children through rubbings, which are really a form of printing. This lesson is about representing textures in drawing. It is easier for children to draw textures if they collect a range of marks that can represent textured surfaces.

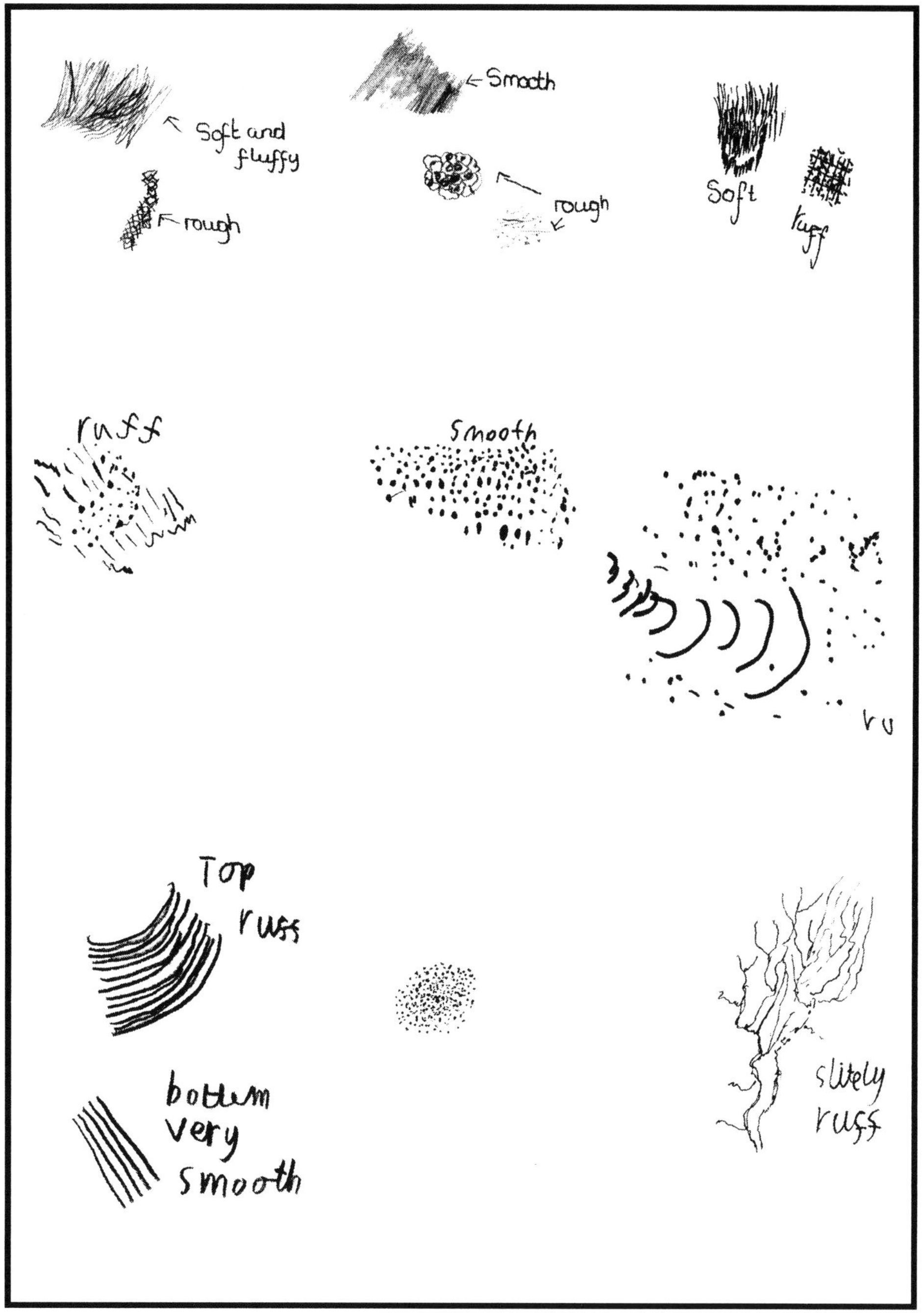

Examples of different textures drawn by Year 4 children

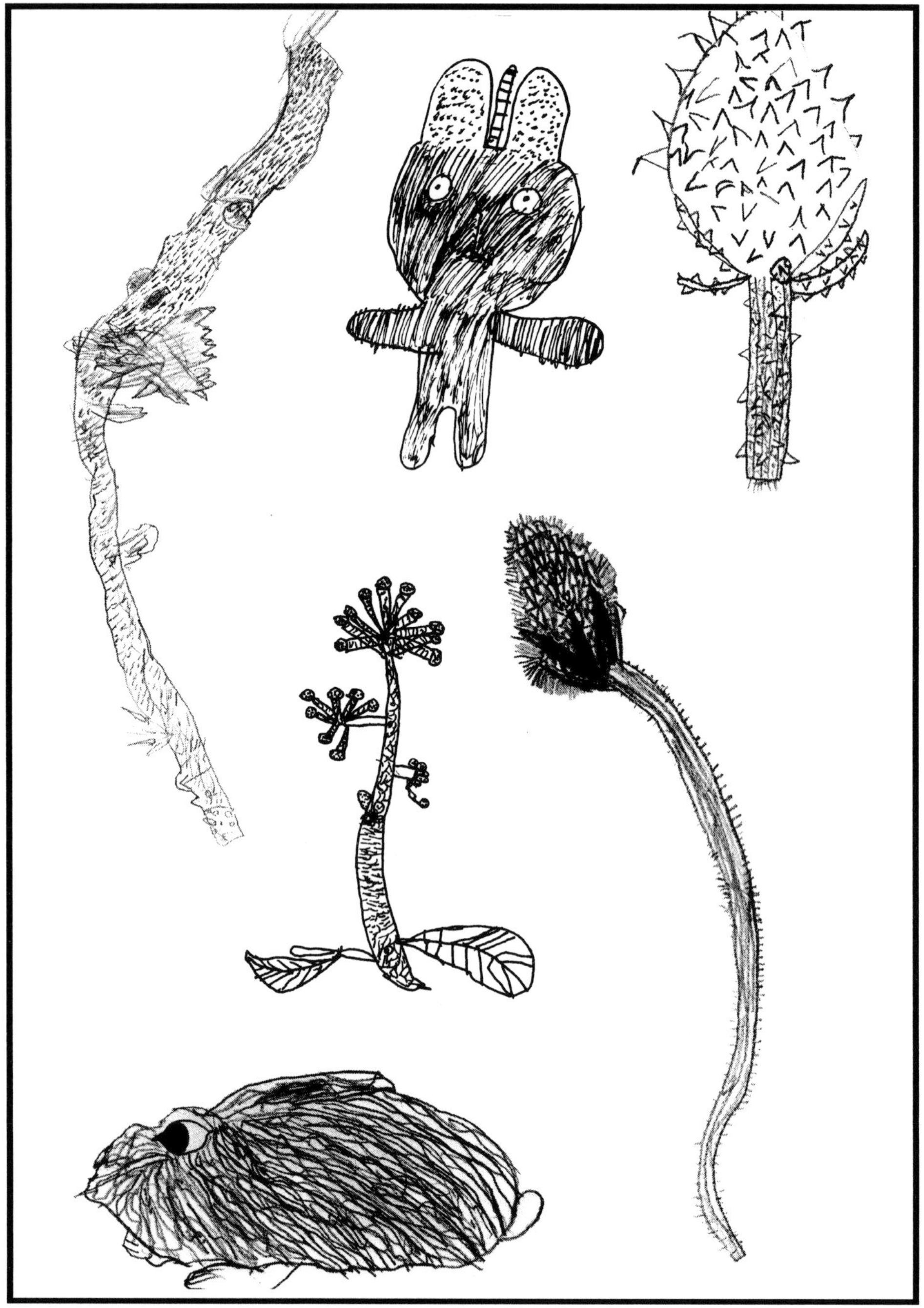

Drawing textures

Time	Resources	National Curriculum
30 min.	Sketchbooks Variety of media: B or 2B pencils, ball-point pens, fine line pens, crayons, charcoal (all black if possible) Artefacts with textured surfaces: shells, rope, twigs with bark, brushes, and mossy stone (see list on page 69) Children could draw themselves or each other	1a, 1c, 2a, 2b, 2c, 4a

A collection of drawings by Year 3 children showing textures

Introduction

'Using texture in your drawings can help to make them more interesting to look at. Today in your drawing you will be concentrating on including all the different textures you can see.'

Practical activity

- ❐ Put a selection of different drawing media on the tables.
- ❐ Children discuss with a partner the textures of items to be drawn, and the media that would be most suitable for the subject matter.
- ❐ Suggest that they might want to use more than one drawing medium within the same drawing to achieve a particular effect.
- ❐ Also suggest they could shade with the side of the pencil and then add marks over the top.
- ❐ Children now do a quick light line drawing of the subject.
- ❐ Then they draw in as many different textures as they can see, using whatever marks they think appropriate.

Background information

You may need to demonstrate how to represent different textures such as fur, woven fabric or hair with different marks, for example by using dots, dashes and overlapping wavy lines. If they are drawing themselves or each other, bring their attention to all the different textures: skin, different clothing fabrics or hair. Point out that very short hair has a different texture from long or curly hair; that leather shoes have a different texture from fabric trainers. If the different drawing media are the same colour, children will find it easier to focus on the character of the medium.

Pattern

Wesley Knowler, Year 4 (pen drawing of Cholmondeley Sisters 1600-10)

Rationale

Pattern is an element of drawing that children tend to really enjoy. They can lose themselves in making patterns. They take pleasure in watching the lines and shapes gradually spread across the page. They feel a sense of achievement as the pattern develops, and while they are drawing they can day-dream a little. Day-dreaming is an essential element of creativity.

Investigating and making patterns is one way of developing their aesthetic sensibilities.

Jordan Clark's designs for didgeridoos

What is pattern?

Pattern is a repeat of lines, shapes or colours. Pattern falls roughly into three groups: regular, irregular and unintentional pattern.

Pattern in nature, regular and irregular
Pattern in nature is often irregular, like the spots on a leopard. In the case of the leopard's spots or the tiger's stripes, there is a family of shapes. We perceive them as patterns but they are in fact irregular.

Other patterns in nature are regular in shape but they vary in size, such as the whorls on a tortoise shell, the scales on a fish or the feathers on a bird.

Single shapes such as the spiral on a shell can be taken and turned into a pattern. It can be the inspiration for a pattern, but on its own it is not a pattern.

Regular patterns
Regular patterns are more likely to be man-made. They are made by regular repeats of lines, shapes or colours.

The simplest pattern will consist of a single shape, line or colour, repeated in a regular way.

More complex patterns use more than one shape, line or colour. They might repeat in different ways, such as by rotating, reflecting or inverting motifs.

Unintentional pattern
Cars in a car park, books on shelves, leaves in a pile, products on supermarket shelves – because they are in families of shapes they create a kind of pattern.

Pattern for decoration

Pattern is closely associated with the decorative arts – tiles, pottery, fabrics, wallpaper, tapestries, carpets – and also with folk art. From earliest times people have felt the need to decorate artefacts. Cultural traditions and fashions have defined styles, while materials and tools available have influenced the types of patterns produced.

Patterns are designed to fit the objects they are going to decorate; plate designs tend to be round, borders long and narrow.

Collecting, analyzing and creating patterns lead very naturally to print-making. Although in this chapter patterns will be drawn, the work will still be a very useful foundation for printing.

About this chapter

Artists are inspired by pattern in nature, so it is a good starting point for children. We are surrounded by pattern in the natural and man-made world, so there is plenty of scope for stimulus.

In this chapter children will study how simple patterns are made from line and shape and how to add to these in different ways to make them more complex.

They will study both regular and irregular patterns in nature, and those used in the art and craft of different cultures.

They will develop a bank of patterns that they can apply later to designs.

Year 4 child's drawing in pen and water colour

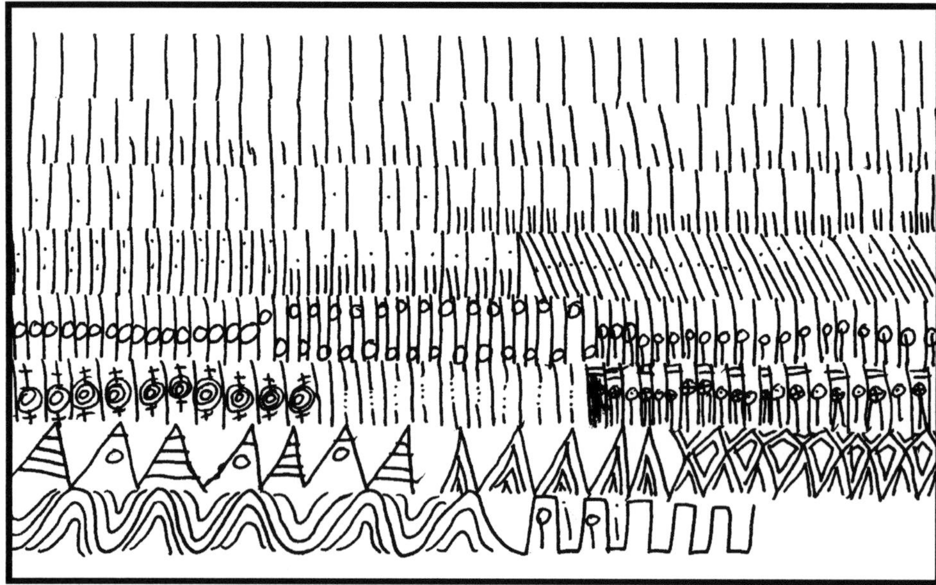
Year 3 child's simple line and shape patterns

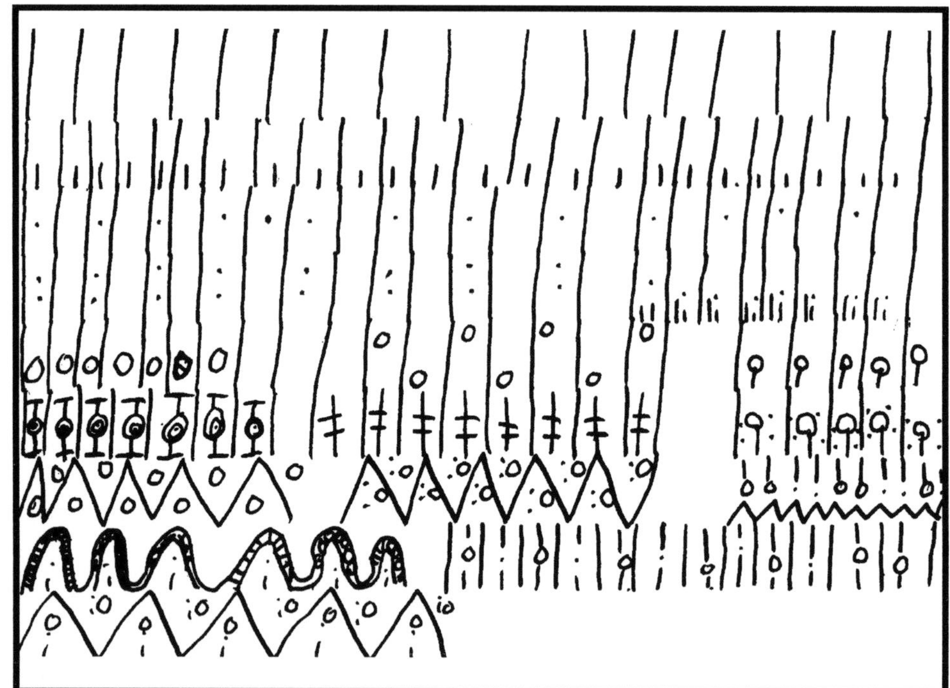
Year 3 child's simple line and shape patterns

Making patterns with line and shape 1

Time	Resources	National Curriculum
30 min.	Sketchbooks Any pencil, HB will do (could use felt tips) Large piece of white paper for teacher modelling	4a

Introduction

'Pattern is made up of repeated lines or shapes. You are going to make some simple patterns, then you will add to these to make them more complicated.'

Practical activity

(Model each stage.)

- Children draw short straight lines, the same size and the same space apart, across the paper.

  | | | | | | |

- Now try a long line, a short line, long line, short line, etc.

  | | | | | |

- Next try a line and a dot. Repeat across page.

  |. |. |. |.

- Explain that it is important that the spaces between the lines are always the same size.
- Children could now try two short lines, one long line, repeated.

  || | || | || | || |

- ❒ Two lines, two dots, repeated.
- ❒ One line, one circle, repeated.
- ❒ They should now be able to make up some of their own.
- ❒ They could include shapes (squares, triangles, circles) within squares.
- ❒ Suggest zig-zags, waves, keys. Adding dots to any of these extends the variety.

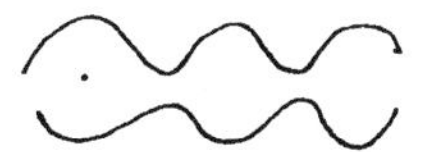

Potential pitfall!
Children tend to disregard spacing when creating patterns. Emphasize that spaces are as important as the motif.

Background information
This activity is closely related to handwriting and helps improve hand–eye co-ordination. Once they have grasped the concept of a pattern being a regular repeat they can work on a smaller scale.

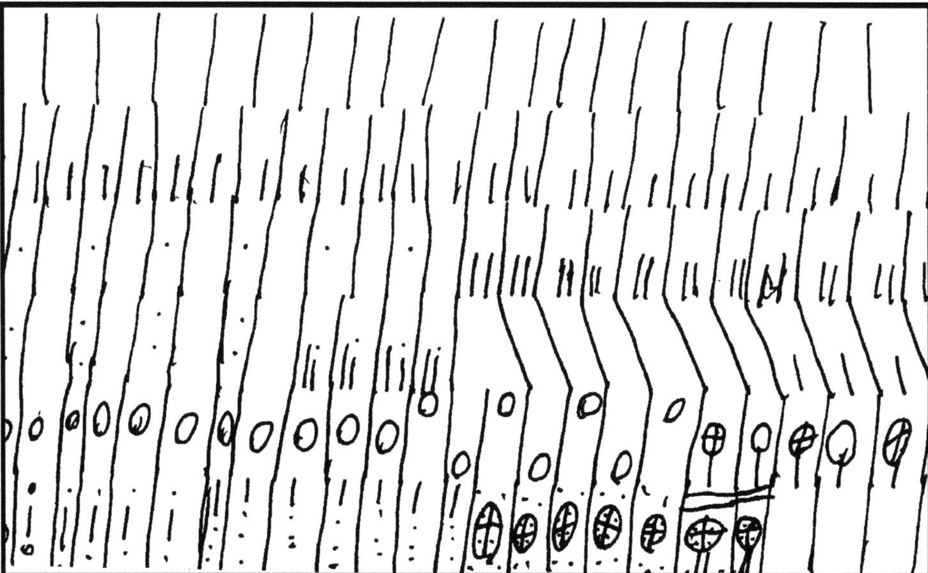

Year 3 child's simple line and shape patterns

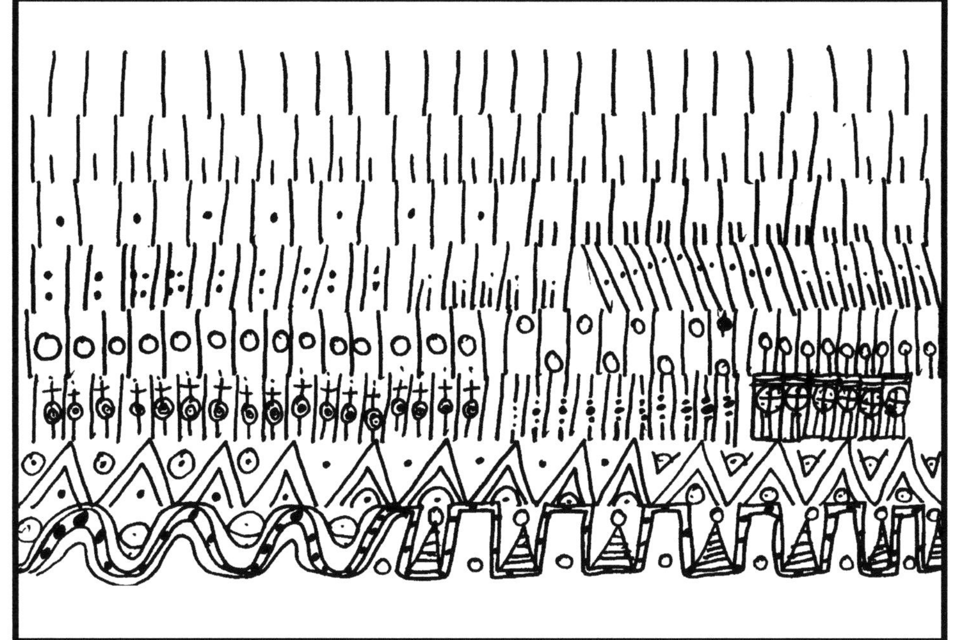

Year 3 child's simple line and shape patterns

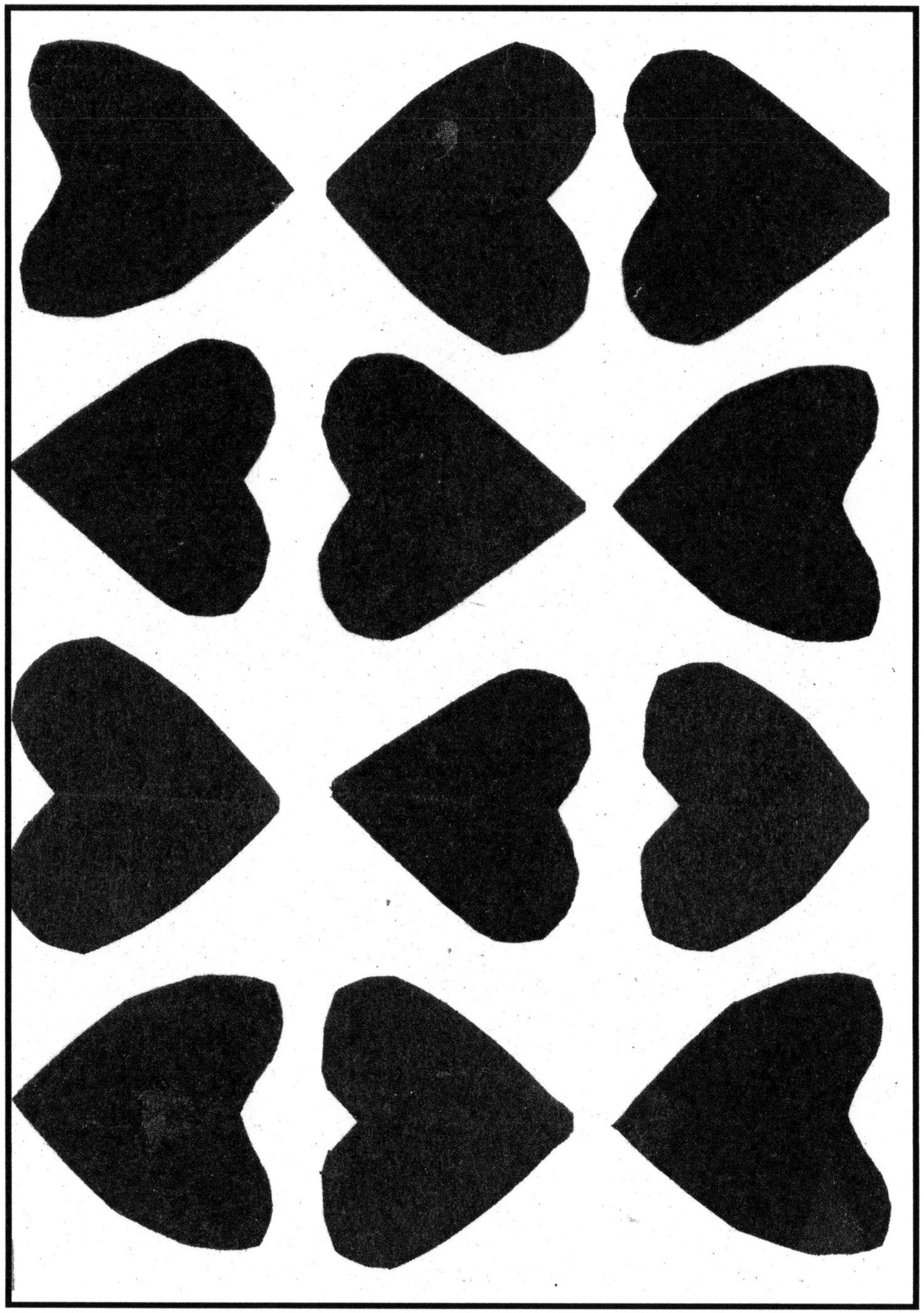

Stage 1, showing shapes stuck in position

Making patterns with line and shape 2

Time	Resources	National Curriculum
30–40 min.	A3 paper, white or coloured Pencils or felt tips Coloured paper, A5 approx. Glue Scissors	1c, 3b, 4a

Although the focus of the chapter is about drawing patterns, it is easier for children to understand rotated and reflected repeats if they experiment with cut paper first. This activity will also help when they use patterns in printing.

Introduction

'Pattern is made by regularly repeating shapes, lines and colours. You have tried some patterns which include lines and shapes. Now you are going to see what happens if you turn the shapes in different ways.'

Practical activity

❒ Demonstrate on the board what happens if you rotate a shape such as a heart.

❒ Ask children to choose a shape such as a heart, flower, diamond or cross.

❒ They fold the coloured paper as many times as they can but so it can still easily be cut through.

❒ Now they draw the shape on the paper and cut it out. They will now have a number of shapes.

❒ Children arrange them on a piece of background paper in three or four rows. Don't stick them down yet!

- ❐ Next they turn alternate shapes upside down.
- ❐ Suggest trying different combinations: two up, two down, or all up one row, all down the next.
- ❐ Try rotating the shape through 90 degrees. Or turn half the shapes over, if they are not symmetrical.
- ❐ Once children have the idea they will be able to come up with many different arrangements.
- ❐ They can add in another shape, or the same shape in a different colour.
- ❐ Remind them that the spaces between the shapes must be regular.
- ❐ When they have finished, they should stick their design down and add some lines.

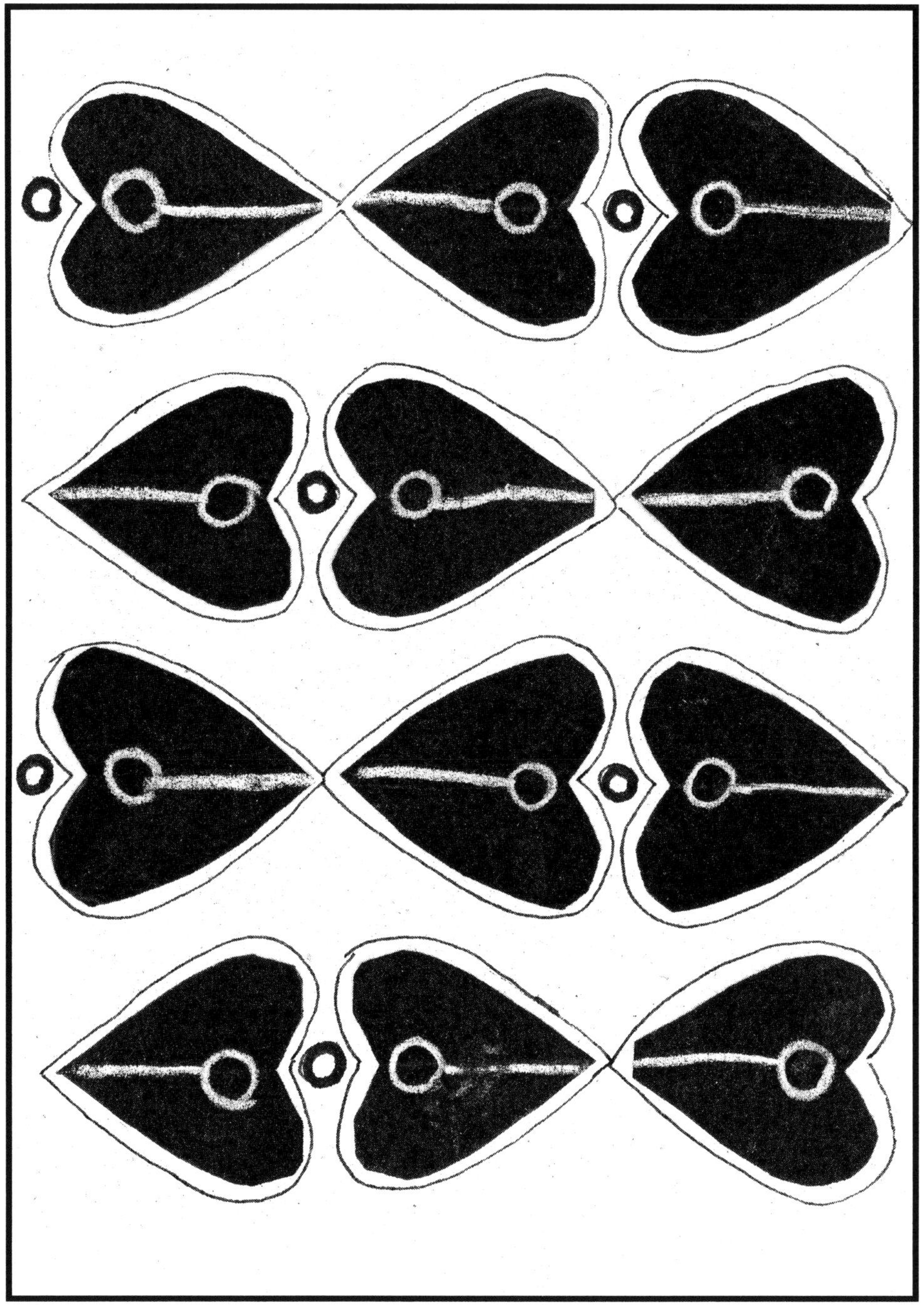

Stage 2, showing shape pattern with lines added

Using line patterns in a doodle

Time	Resources	National Curriculum
15 min. to set up doodle	Sketchbooks/paper Fine felt tips or fine line pens Resource sheet 10 (page 138)	4a

Introduction

'Today you are going to create some doodles.' (Show them some doodles done by other children. If you have no examples, use the example on page 61 and Resource sheet 10. These were originally A3, so enlarge them if possible.) *'All these doodles started with a small shape in the middle and grew very, very slowly over some weeks. This is mostly a line pattern activity, so no solid colouring in.'*

Practical activity

- ❒ Start the doodle in the middle of the paper, by drawing a simple shape such as a heart, cross, flower, square or circle.

- ❒ Add different small lines and shapes to the motif.

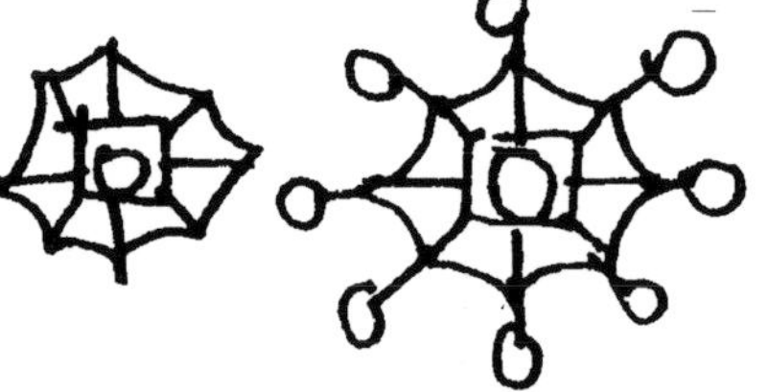
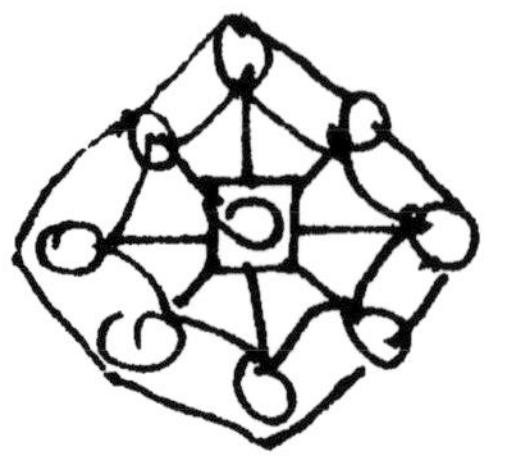

- ❒ Explain that every time their lines create a shape they should fill that shape in with a pattern. They could look back in their sketchbooks at their handwriting and line patterns for ideas.
- ❒ Remind them to work slowly and carefully.
- ❒ Once started, the doodles can be done in odd moments, for example, clearing-up time or during registration.

Potential pitfall!

Children are inclined to rush to cover the page in one session. Suggest that after 10 minutes the doodle should be no bigger than a 50p piece. A little solid colouring looks good, but too much will wreck the pens.

Background information

Looking at pattern is an essential part of learning to draw. Creating patterns can be a very pleasing activity. As the patterns grow, so do the children's confidence and their aesthetic appreciation of pattern.

Children can build up their own collections of line patterns over a period of time. They can then use them to decorate other pieces of work, or they can turn the collections of patterns into works of art in their own right. Once children have a bank of patterns, they can launch into decorative art and craft activities with greater confidence.

Hettie Pearson, Year 4

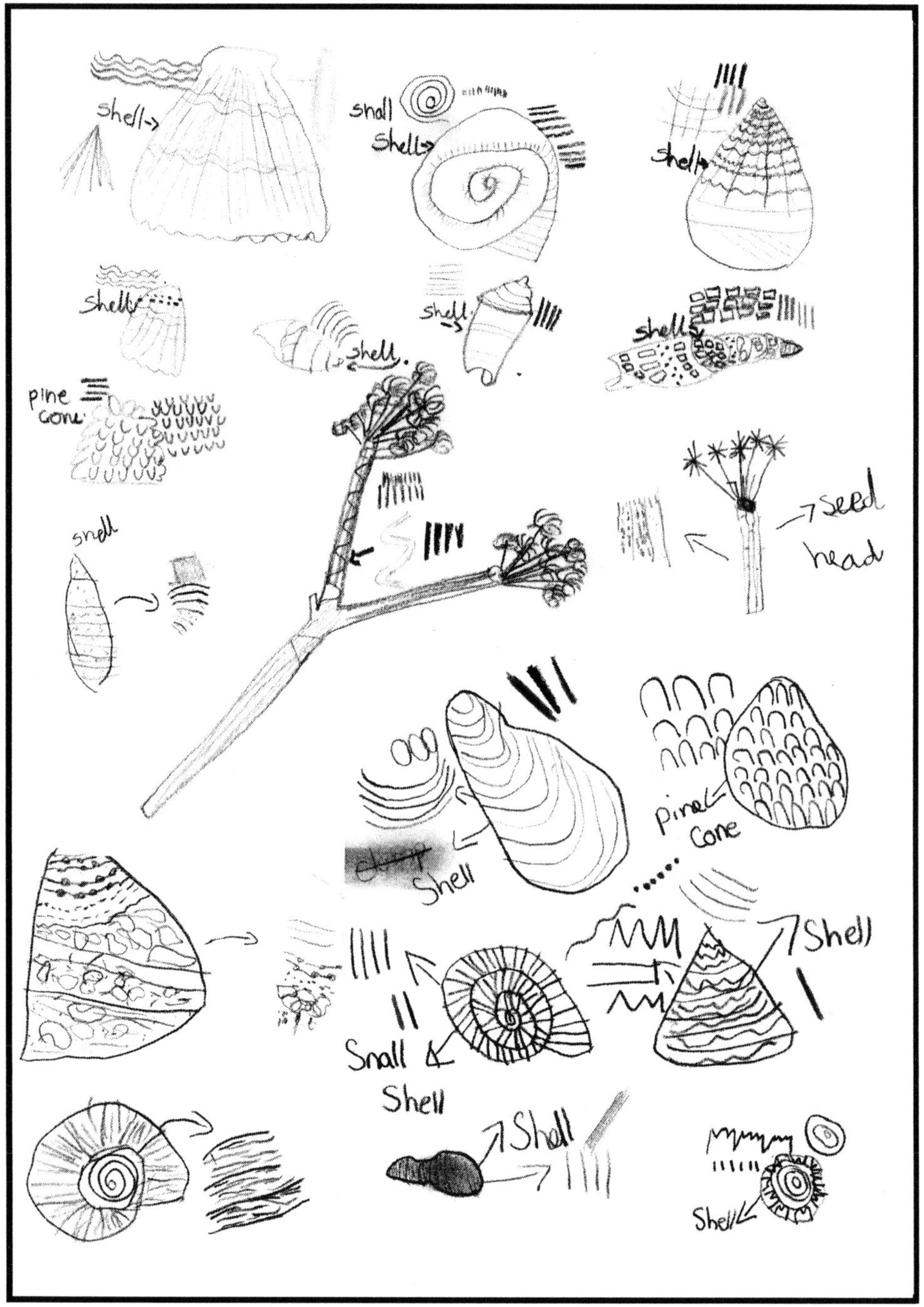

Year 3 child's drawing of natural artefacts and the patterns found on each

Collecting patterns from nature

Time	Resources	National Curriculum
30–40 min.	Sketchbooks B pencils Selection of natural artefacts that have patterns: shells, leaves, fruit, vegetables, feathers (see list on page 69) Magnifying glasses Large piece of white paper for teacher modelling	1a, 1b, 1c, 4a

Introduction

'You can find lots of patterns in the world around us. Patterns are repeats of lines, shapes or colours. You can see patterns in waves in the sea, clouds in the sky or in a leaf. These are natural patterns. If there is a single shape or line, like the spiral on a shell, it is not a pattern. It could become one if you copied and repeated it. You are going to look very closely at some natural patterns using the magnifying glasses.'

Practical activity

- ❒ Distribute the artefacts so there is a variety on each table.
- ❒ Encourage children to talk about the patterns they can see, and draw a few of the patterns on a large piece of paper or the board, e.g. the arrangement of dots from the seed head, some lines from the leaf, and so on.
- ❒ Children draw an object quickly, and then draw just the patterns and label them, e.g. 'Pattern from inside an orange'.
- ❒ It might be useful to make a few notes about the colour for future reference, for example for a weaving or print.
- ❒ Children should draw as many different objects and patterns as there is time for.

Background information
Collections of patterns in sketchbooks are an invaluable resource. Children can use the patterns at some later time for decorating something, or for a project that is already in hand. For example: printing, indenting patterns on clay, or decorating a papier mâché plate.

'Much of learning to draw consists of discovering how things appear rather than how they are, and it is not until we begin to draw that most of us discover the tremendous difference between what we know about objects and what we see.'
Daniel Mendelowitz, Drawing: A Study Guide

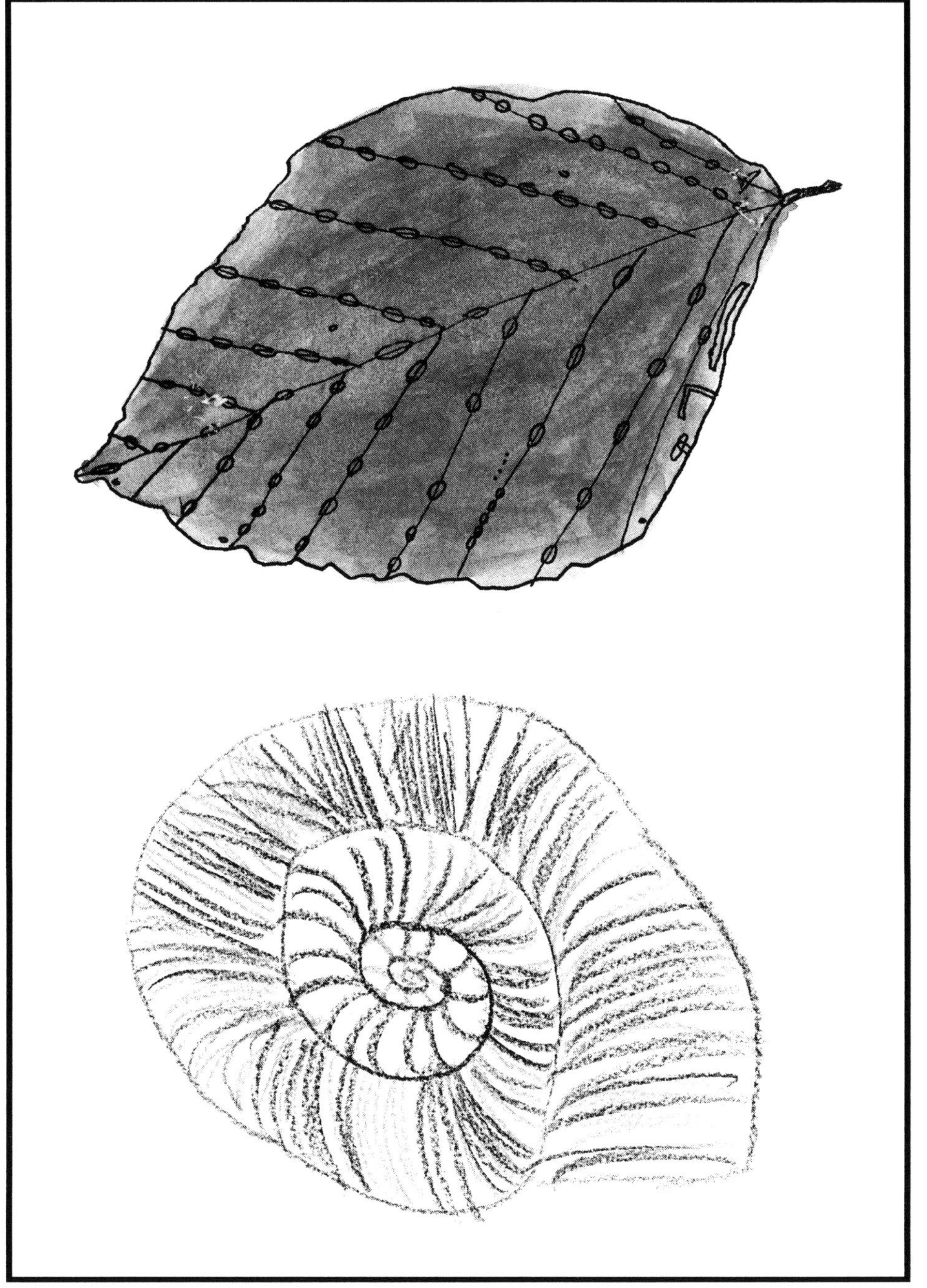

Shell by Jack Perham, Year 3; leaf by Daisy Perham, Year 4

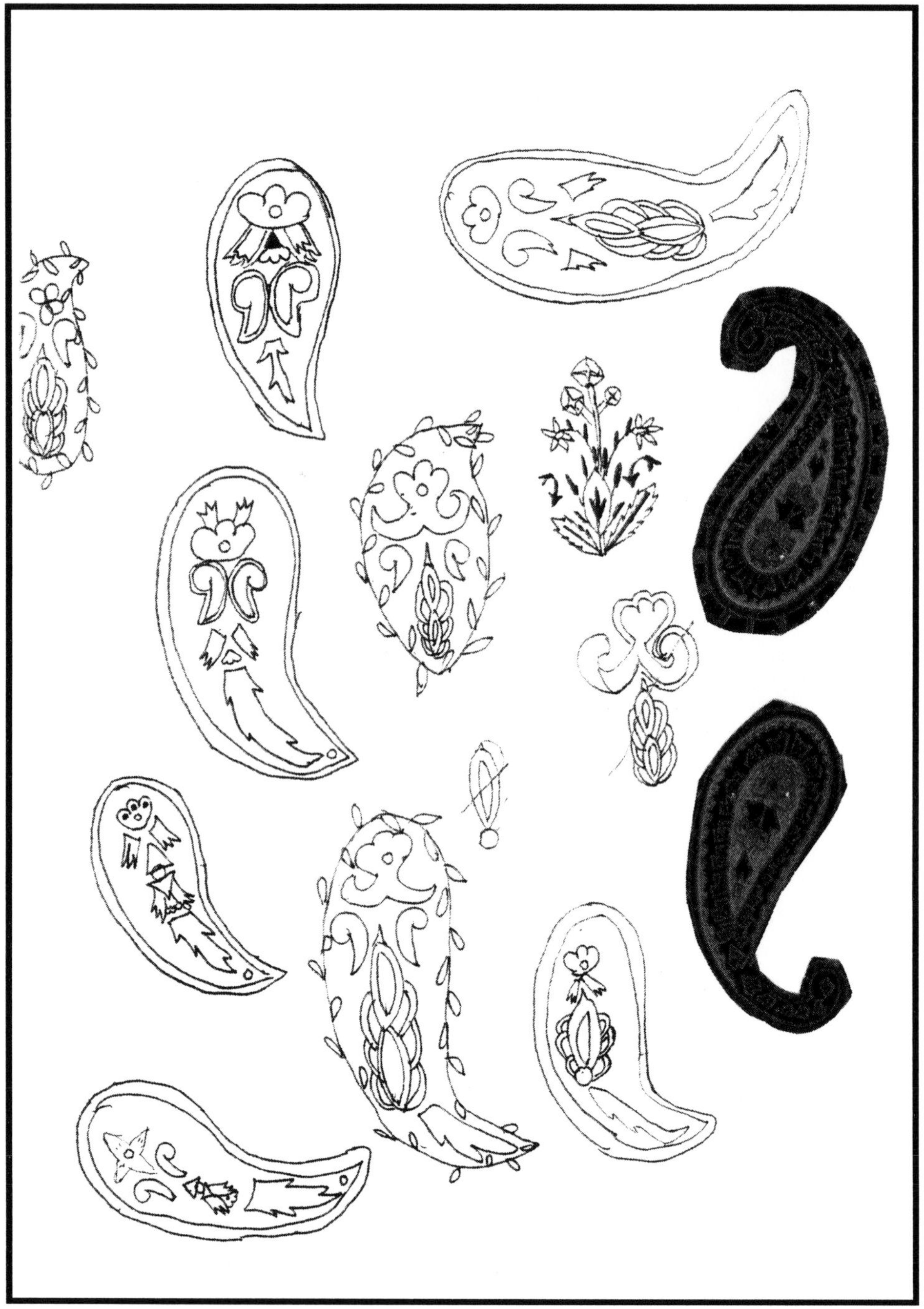

Year 4 child's drawing of different paisley patterns found on fabrics and fabric cuttings

Collecting patterns from different cultures

Time	Resources	National Curriculum
30–40 min.	Sketchbooks Pencils or fine pens Collection of artefacts relating to culture being studied (could be fabrics, weavings, pottery or carvings) Large piece of white paper for teacher modelling	1a, 1b, 4a, 4b, 5a, 5d

Introduction

'Ideas for patterns often come from nature, like the paisley leaf in Indian designs. Some are traditional and have been used for decoration for many years. You are going to look at these artefacts and draw some of the patterns that have been used.'

Practical activity

- ❒ Share out the objects.
- ❒ Choose a pattern or motif that has been repeated and draw it on a large piece of paper or the board as an example.
- ❒ Children copy as many different patterns as they can find.
- ❒ They could label them and perhaps make notes about the colours used.
- ❒ Explain that this might be useful later, as they could use the patterns as a starting point for prints or a weaving.

Example of Year 3 child's print using paisley pattern

Melissa Orton, Year 3

Looking

> 'The effort to see things without distortion takes something very like courage and this courage is essential to the artist who has to look at everything as though he saw it for the first time.'
>
> *Henri Matisse, from John Elderfield, The Drawings of Henri Matisse*

Why looking skills are so important

A great deal of curriculum time is given to the development of speaking and listening skills, but looking skills are overlooked. In order that drawing can be developed to the highest quality, children have to learn how to focus their whole attention on whatever it is they are drawing. Through this they will find that the longer and more concentrated the focus of attention, the more they will see.

Informed looking is very useful across the curriculum:

- In maths it develops awareness of shapes and angles, and the ability to recognize patterns
- In science it develops children's abilities to make deductions about materials
- In history children are better able to make hypotheses by looking at and handling artefacts, and by looking at historical locations and photographs
- In geography they are able to make deductions from looking at different aspects of landscapes.

Learning to draw is really a matter of learning to see. This sounds so simple. If it were simple then we would all be able to draw without needing to be taught or teach ourselves. Through learning to draw, children learn to look, and they need to look with specific intent to be able to draw well.

'Drawing is not really very difficult, seeing is the problem.'
Betty Edwards,
Drawing on the Right Side of the Brain

This chapter identifies the different skills of looking that are essential for success in drawing.

Rationale

'The ability to see and the ability to draw are closely related. When we are young our seeing, drawing, reading and writing develop alongside each other, but there is an emphasis in our society on literacy and the ability to comprehend mathematical concepts. As the teaching in these subjects propels us forwards, our ability to communicate in visual terms remains underdeveloped.'
Ian Simpson, Drawing, Seeing and Observing

Learning to look carefully at the subject you are drawing is as important as, if not more important than, learning to use different media and rules about proportions. We need to help children to draw what they see, not what they think they can see. Children need help with knowing what to look for, in their subject and in their drawings, and what to do about what they see.

When the cry goes up: *'My drawing's going all wrong'* they need to know what to do about it. If they are not given enough support there is a considerable tendency, particularly among older primary children, to give up. They rapidly gain the mistaken impression that they cannot draw.

Precision in drawing what you see is partly a matter of practice, but the learning process can be supported and enhanced through certain checking techniques and modes of looking.

Moving on from Key Stage 1

Finding out how things really look is a gradual process helped on by investigating and recording impressions. At Key Stage 1 children are drawing as much by what they know as by what they see. Their drawing is often narrative and they rely on memory or schema to communicate visually.

They will have developed schema with varying degrees of success. A typical schema is that of a landscape, where the sky is a horizontal blue strip at the top of the paper with a similar green one at the base to represent the ground. The sun is often a quarter circle in one upper corner of the page. There are schemas for figures, houses, trees and animals and they serve the child's purpose very well. They are as recognizable as the word 'house' or 'person' and are relatively easy to produce time and time again (see page 11).

These schemas rarely overlap. Objects are drawn facing the child as if they are lined up to be seen and the most important subject matter is drawn largest.

'Children who learn to look learn to question. Children who learn to look begin to understand. Children who learn to look discover.'
Roger Cole, Drawing with Children

'There is only one way to learn to draw and that is a perfectly natural way. It has only to do with the act of correct observation, and by that I mean physical contact with all sorts of objects through all the senses.'
Kimon Nicolaides, The Natural Way to Draw

However, there comes a time when children need to start to take another look, a careful, close, thoughtful look, and to do this most children will need guidance and encouragement.

Children's perception changes at different ages and this often relates to their maturity. The less able child will often cling to their schema because it is secure and gives them a degree of success and they know how their drawing will turn out. Abandoning schema and drawing by looking, touching and hypothesizing about the subject matter is both exciting and frightening. Suddenly drawings don't go as expected, drawing gets to be a bit of a struggle and results can be disappointing.

Children can be supported through this stage and the development of their perception encouraged in various ways. (See 'About this chapter', page 68).

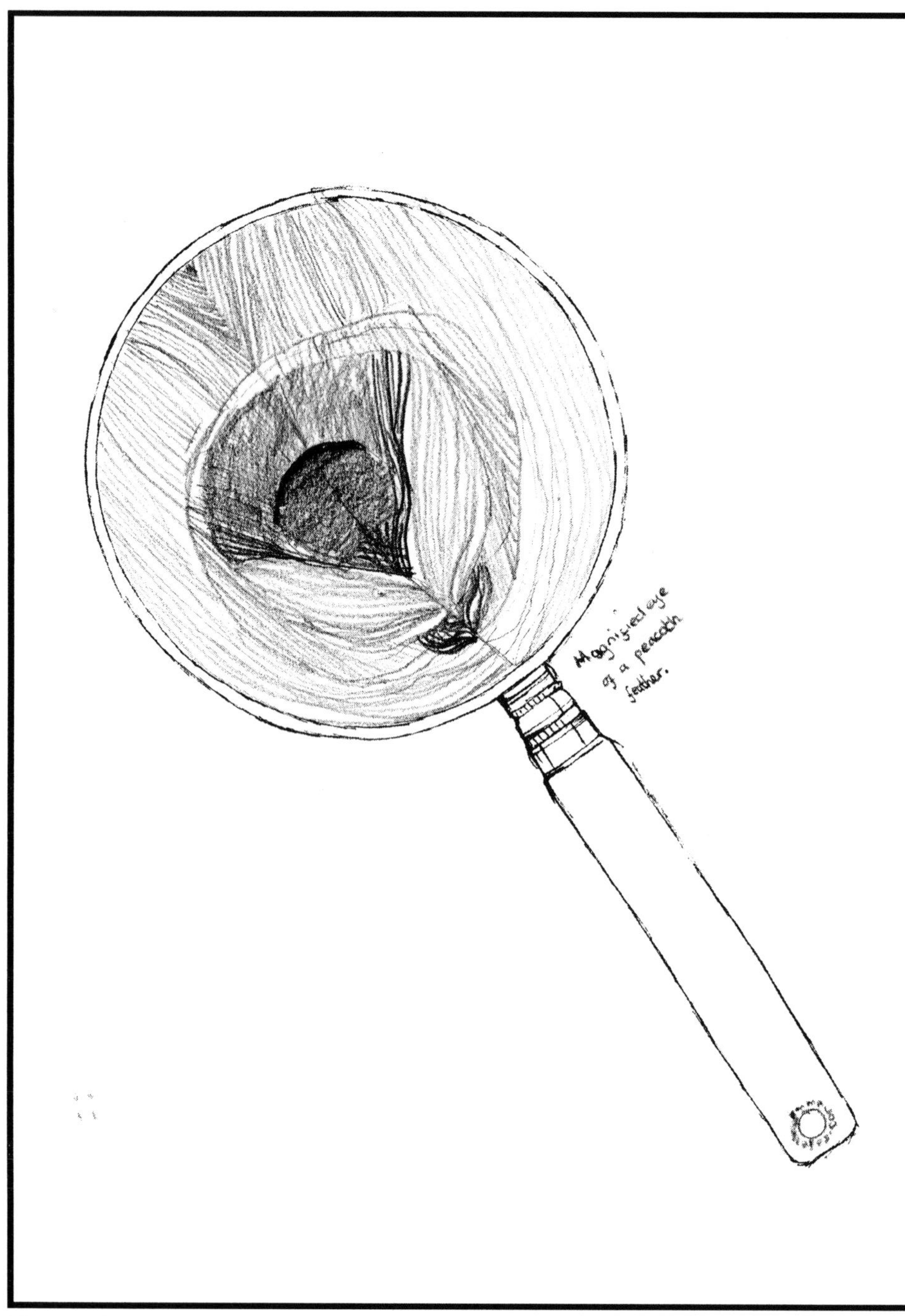

Year 4 child's drawing of magnified eye of a peacock feather

About this chapter

In this chapter children will be encouraged to look in a variety of ways:

- ❐ They will learn to look with curiosity
- ❐ Their looking will be engaged by talking about the subjects, by questioning and hypothesizing
- ❐ They will collect a descriptive vocabulary
- ❐ They will have contact with the subject matter through as many senses as possible, especially through the sense of touch
- ❐ They will use focusing devices such as magnifying glasses, mirrors and viewfinders
- ❐ They will have practice in drawing and comparing shapes and judging their accuracy
- ❐ They will learn to see the overall shape of a subject, and to start by drawing it lightly
- ❐ They will learn to recognize and draw right angles and parallel lines
- ❐ They will learn to recognize negative shapes and to understand how they can use their awareness of them to improve their drawings
- ❐ They will learn the technique of sighting and how to make comparative judgements about shapes and proportions.

List of possible subjects for drawing or discussion

Natural
Flowers
Leaves
Buds
Seeds
Seedheads
Bulbs
Sprouting beans
Grasses
Moss
Branches
Twigs
Bark
Roots
Seaweed
Shells
Dried starfish
Seahorses
Sea urchins
Crab shells
Wasps' nests
Pebbles
Fossils
Feathers
Nuts
Fruit
Vegetables
Quartz
Crystals

Man-made
Carvings
Jewellery
Embroidery
Tools
Kitchen tools
Kitchen equipment, e.g. egg whisks, colanders, tin openers, etc.
Locks
Shoes
Hats
Umbrellas
Science equipment
Pottery
Historial artefacts
Ethnic artefacts
Toys
Rope
Nets
Gardening tools
Watering cans
Brooms and brushes
Vacuum cleaners
Mops and buckets
Musical instruments
Bikes
Roller blades
Rollerskates

Workings or insides of
(broken and/or switched off!)
Clocks
Locks
Circuits
Radios
Televisions
Computers
Telephones
Engines
Engine parts
Clockwork toys
Wheels
Cogs

Animals
Alive
Minibeasts
Tadpoles
Small pets
Ants in ant colony
Worms in wormery

Dead
Stuffed animals
Stuffed birds
Stuffed fish
Mounted insects
Mounted butterflies

'For merely looking at an object cannot be of any use to us. All looking goes into observing, all observing into reflecting, all reflecting into connecting, and so one can say that with every attentive look we cast into the world we are already theorising.'
Attributed to Johann Wolfgang von Goethe

How drawing is affected by the two halves of the brain

This topic is covered in much more detail in the Years 5–6 book. Year 3 and 4 children might like to hear a little about it (particularly in relation to the lesson on Looking and drawing from different viewpoints (see pages 92–93).

The following two paragraphs can be read to them:

> As seen from above, your brain resembles the two halves of a walnut. These two halves are called the left and right hemispheres. The left side is dominant. It deals with knowledge, language and labelling, logic and order, numbers, time and symbols. It is the side that gets the most exercise in school.
>
> The right side is intuitive; it senses things, it makes connections but doesn't jump to conclusions, it sees likenesses between things and it deals with insight. It understands spatial relationships. The right side of the brain is one side we need to use when we are drawing.

How the eyes and brain work together

The eyes work in conjuction with the brain. When we look at something, we see a small upside down image. This image is sent to the brain as coded information in the form of electrical impulses. The information is arranged in such a way that to the brain it represents the object.

No image appears in the brain. The coded information acts as a substitute for the object in the same way a word does. So in a way we see what the brain has decided we have seen. The brain is very clever at decoding the information it receives and informing us about the visual world. It uses clues in the absence of complete evidence and so can be deluded by information received and form wrong judgements – rather like detectives jumping to the wrong conclusion from the facts they have gathered.

How the left side of the brain causes problems in drawing

The brain is always trying to find objects in the information it receives from the eyes and it needs very little help in order to produce them. The left side quickly names the objects and then stored knowledge steps in to complete the picture.

When the retina registers a well-known form – a tree, a house, a person or whatever – the left side of the brain immediately names it. Thereupon children need look no further: they know all about houses and people, so the looking stops and knowledge takes over.

'Learning to draw is really a matter of learning to see correctly and that means a good deal more than merely looking with the eye.'
Kimon Nicolaides, The Natural Way to Draw

'As we increase the range of what we see we increase the richness of what we imagine.'
John Ruskin (from Roger Coles, Drawing with Children)

Children are inclined to draw from an internal model that contains central defining facts about the subject. This is why they tend to draw not what they see, but what they know and think they can see. Tree trunks are straight, no need to look, says the left side of the brain, just draw it. The trunk may actually be curved or divided, but this passes unnoticed. Taking another look seems almost like arguing with what they know. People have a head, arms, legs, feet, etc. The fact that in a particular pose the feet are hidden from view is easily overlooked. The left side of the brain knows all about people and will supply all the information, so it can cause children to draw something that they cannot see. Children draw from memorized, stored drawing symbols, which are no longer appropriate to the task.

They need to learn to trust what they actually do see, to switch off the left side of the brain and let the right side take over. This is not easy, as the left side (partly because it gets so much more exercise than the right side) is dominant.

Year 3 children's drawings of a chair was placed on a table. The seat was not visible, nevertheless the children drew it as they knew it was there.

How to develop the right side of the brain
One way is to set a task that the left side cannot do or doesn't understand. The left side doesn't like looking at negative shapes as it can't name them, so drawing negative shapes is a good exercise.

The left side doesn't like seeing things from unusual angles as it cannot jump to conclusions so easily. Therefore, drawing things upside down is a good exercise for the right side.

The left side dislikes drawing slowly, having to keep the eyes constantly on the subject, so children will be recording minutely what is seen but not thinking about what the object is. This is another activity which gives the right side a chance to take over. Looking and holding a mental picture of what is seen and then drawing that bit involves a shift between the left and right side, which is ideal.

'When I eat a tomato I look at it in the same way as anyone else would, but when I paint a tomato then I see it very differently.'

Henri Matisse (from John Elderfield, The Drawings of Henri Matisse)

Focusing looking through talking

Time	Resources	National Curriculum
30 min.	Interesting objects that children can relate to (see list on page 69) These could be topic-led, or part of the school equipment, natural or man-made	4a

This activity can be done in relation to several other curriculum areas, such as science, history or design and technology.

Introduction

'In order to draw something well you need to spend time looking carefully at it before you begin to draw. Careful looking before you start to draw will make a huge difference to your drawings. The key to drawing lies in the eyes, not as you might think in the hands. You are going to be looking at, touching (if this is possible) *and talking about these objects. Then you will draw them.'*

Practical activity

Ask questions to engage children's looking:

❐ What shape is it?
❐ Can you see any other shapes?
❐ Is it soft or hard? What words would you use to describe the way it feels?
❐ Do you notice any rough/smooth/shiny/sharp/spiky/fluffy parts?
❐ What is the widest/narrowest/thickest/thinnest part of it?
❐ What is the lightest/darkest part of it?
❐ Does it look the same if I turn it over?
❐ What is this part for?
❐ How does it join on to this bit?
❐ Does it have a smell?
❐ What does the smell remind you of?
❐ How does it sound if you tap/rattle/wind/shake/drop/spin it/scrape a nail over it?
❐ What do you think it is made of?
❐ Is it all made of the same material?
❐ Is it bigger than: You? This? That?
❐ Is it heavy or light?
❐ Do you think it is old or new?

Background information

The purpose of this activity is to involve the children with the subject, to help them see things they might not otherwise notice. Initially the describing could be done by the teacher to model the type of vocabulary and the range of observations possible.

These are some of the aspects of a subject that could be described:

❐ The overall shape
❐ Smaller shapes within the main outline
❐ Colours
❐ Textures
❐ Darkest and lightest areas
❐ Patterns
❐ Sounds or smells
❐ Comparative lengths and breadths
❐ Curves or angles
❐ Reflections
❐ Small details such as markings, lettering, screws, stitching
❐ The purpose or origin of the item
❐ How it was created or made, where and by whom
❐ How it looks from different angles.

When possible, children should have the opportunity to feel the items and describe the textures.

Talking about the subject before drawing

Time	Resources	National Curriculum
45 min. approx.	Sketchbooks Drawing media appropriate to subject matter Interesting objects that children can relate to (see list on page 69)	1a, 2c, 4a, 5a

Follow the pattern for focusing children's looking as covered in the previous lesson. The descriptive vocabulary generated could be written on the board and children could copy it into their sketchbooks with the drawings. Children should have the opportunity to draw the items as soon as possible after the discussion session.

It is quite interesting for them to draw the items first, then do the focusing activity. Having completed this activity, they draw the items again (with new eyes, as it were). The difference in the two sets of drawings can be staggering.

Drawing and discussion times will vary according to the complexity of the subject and the concentration levels of the children.

Practical activities

Version 1

- ❐ Focusing looking through talking activity (on previous page)
- ❐ Draw the objects.

Version 2

- ❐ Draw the objects without prior discussion
- ❐ Focusing looking through talking activity (on previous page)
- ❐ Draw objects again.

Drawn before talking

Drawn after talking

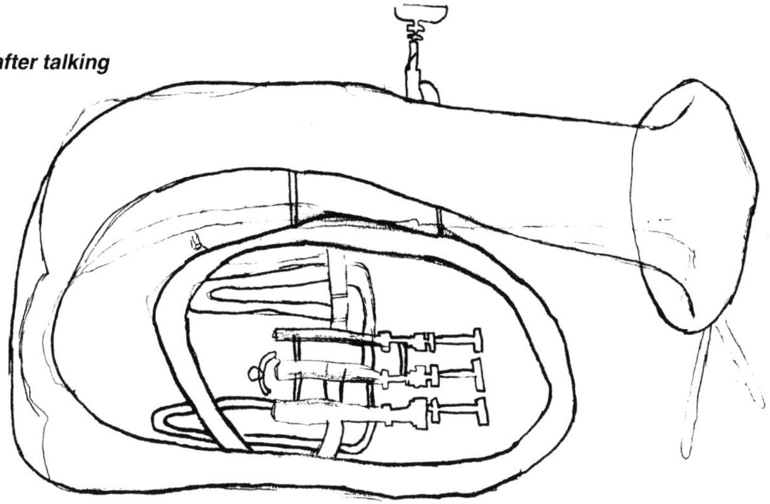

Joe Blackford, Year 4 (drawings done before and after focusing looking activity)

'Children's Games' by Pieter Bruegel (A larger photocopiable version available on page 139). Reproduced with permission from Kunsthistorisches Museum, Vienna

Using focusing devices

Time	Resources	National Curriculum
45 mins. (15 min. per focusing device)	Magnifying glasses (as many as possible) Artefacts suitable for close viewing (see list page 69) Viewfinders (see Background information) Resource sheet 11 (page 139) Plastic mirrors	2c

Practical activities

The different devices can be used on different occasions.

Viewfinders

- ❒ Hand out copies of 'Children's Games' by Pieter Bruegel (Resource sheet 11).
- ❒ Children should lay the viewfinders over an area of the picture and then discuss, report or record what they see.
- ❒ Slide the viewfinder around and select different areas to investigate.
- ❒ This could be done with pictures connected to topics being studied, such as buildings. Children could look at enlarged photographs of streets and find different tiles, doors, window brick patterns, etc.

Mirrors

- ❒ Children could look first at their eyes, inside their mouths, etc.
- ❒ They should then look at a friend's reflection, noting the difference between their usual view of their friend and the reflected view.
- ❒ Children can stand the mirror next to an object and look at its reflection, altering the angle and noting the changes.

Magnifying glasses

- ❒ Magnifying glasses are excellent for investigating the natural world.
- ❒ Children share artefacts and discuss with a partner what they see.
- ❒ Then use magnifying glasses and discuss what they see now.

Background information
Focusing devices help children focus their attention on a subject or areas of a subject they might otherwise overlook. They also help to keep children engaged in looking that little bit longer.

Viewfinders are very useful for focusing children's looking on areas of a complex picture, in order to research subject matter or techniques used. They isolate areas of a subject and are a way of cutting out other visual information that might confuse or distract children. They can be made from stiff card. Black is best as it does not distract the eye from the subject. Cut an aperture (square, rectangular, circular or even keyhole shaped) in the middle of the card.

Magnifying glasses help children notice fine detail and can be used in different ways to enhance their looking.

Mirrors are useful for looking at things from unusual angles and for self-portraits. They can be used in different ways to enhance children's looking.

Year 4 child's pencil self-portrait showing herself viewed from behind holding a mirror

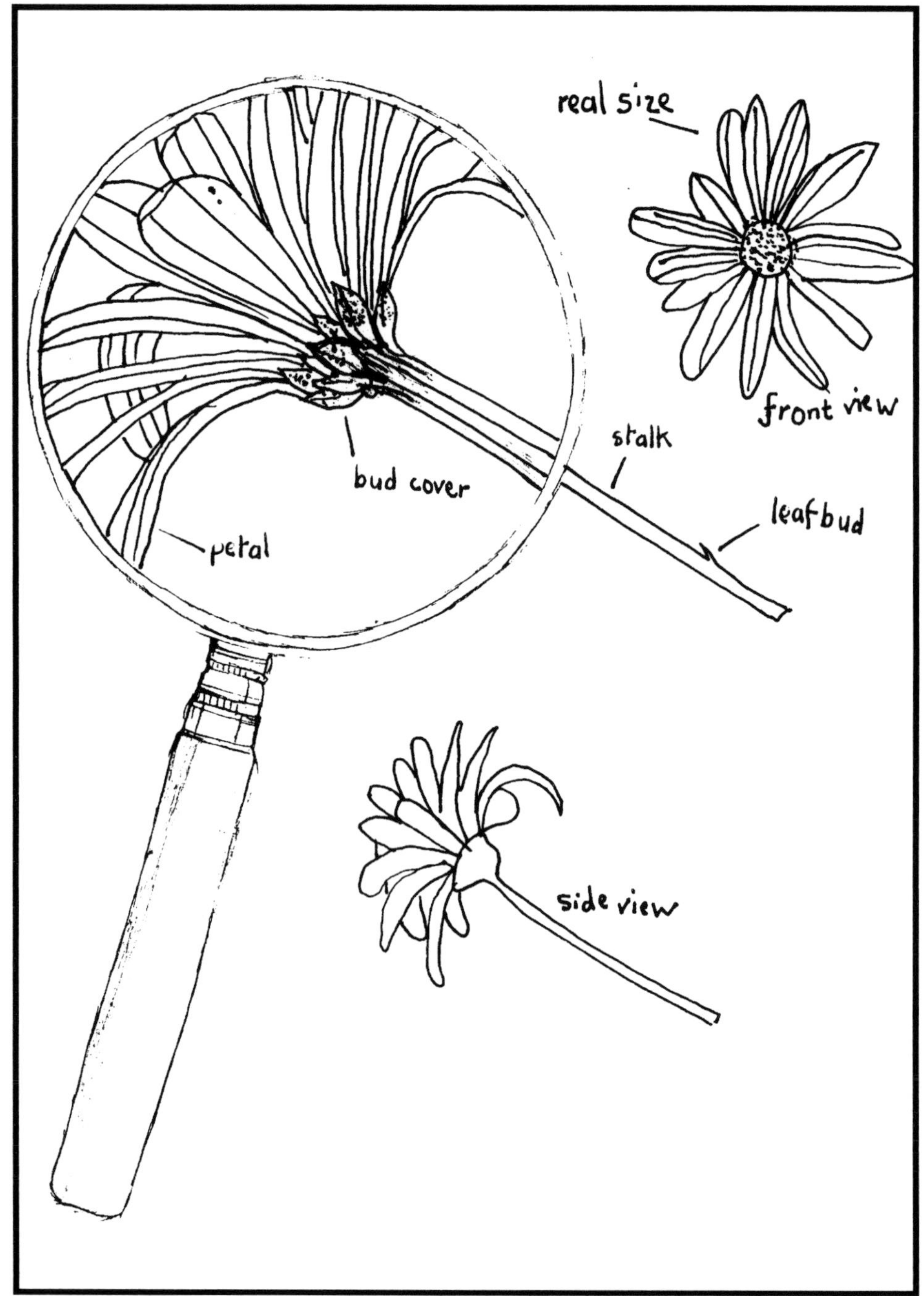

Year 4 child's drawings of a flower from different angles, using a magnifying glass

USING SKILL

Drawing with magnifying glasses

Time	Resources	National Curriculum
30–40 min.	Magnifying glasses, one per child Sketchbooks Drawing pencils or fine line pens Artefacts to draw, topic-related or see list on page 69 Resource sheet 12 (see page 140) – optional	1a, 2c, 4a, 5a

Introduction

'Today you are going to draw (whatever). *Looking carefully before you start will help you create better drawings. We are going to talk about what you can see without the magnifying glasses and then with them. Then you will draw the ... using the magnifying glasses to help you see and draw fine details that you didn't notice before.'* (Give an example.)

Practical activity

- ❒ Spend a few minutes engaging children's looking by talking about shapes and textures (outlined in Focusing looking through talking, on page 72).
- ❒ Encourage children to say what they can see and feel.
- ❒ Children draw the whole artefact and label it.
- ❒ Then they draw a close-up of different parts.
- ❒ They could draw parts of the subject from different angles.
- ❒ They could look at how one part joins onto or grows out of another and how the textures or patterns change from one area to another.
- ❒ They could label different parts of the object, for example: buds, leaves, sepals, petals, stalks, seedheads, patterns on petals, holes or marks made by insects, colour changes, etc.
- ❒ You could give the children a picture of a magnifying glass (Resource sheet 12) for them to draw in what they see.

Background information
Viewfinders and mirrors are excellent focusing devices, but magnifying glasses are probably the most useful device to use in drawing, particularly when drawing and researching from the natural world. It might be a good idea to allow the children to use the magnifying glasses to look at whatever catches their fancy for a few minutes at the beginning of the lesson. They will doubtless look up each other's noses, but it is better they get this out of their systems at the outset, in the hope they won't do it during the lesson!

The glasses could be used in two ways: to look closely at the object before and during drawing the whole of it, or to draw different parts of it.

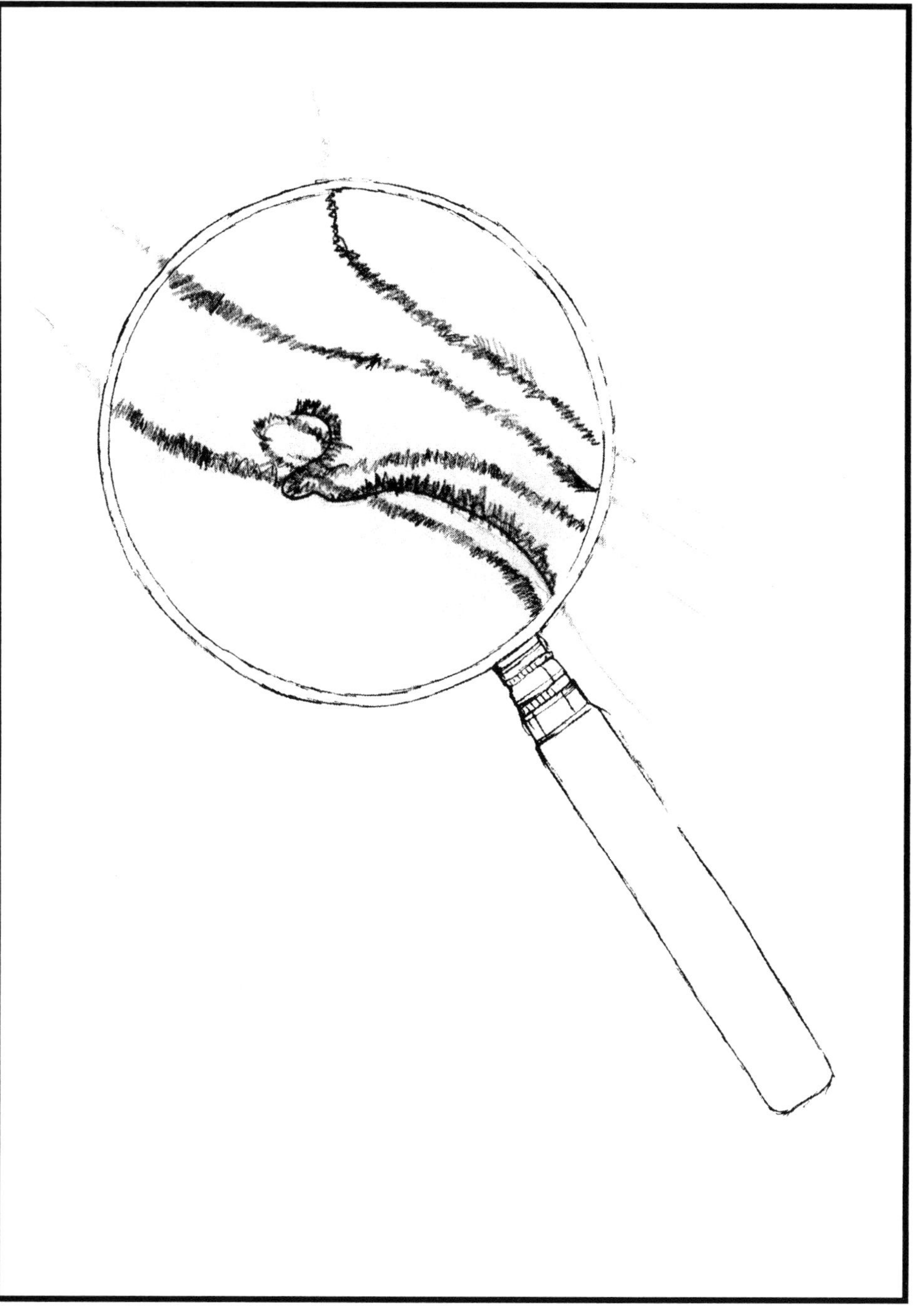

Lemar Bradford, Year 4 (magnified peacock feathers)

Shapes found in everyday objects

Looking for shapes 1

Time	Resources	National Curriculum
15 min. approx.	Artefacts that are simple and easily recognizable in terms of their shape	1a, 4a

Cylinder/ellipse	Sphere/circle	Cuboid/square/rectangle
Bottle	Football	Computer
Bean tin	Teapot	Table
Mug	Pine cone	Cereal packet
Log		Book
Flower pot		Box

Introduction

'You are going to look at some different things that you might draw. First you need to look for the three-dimensinal shape of the whole thing and then for the two-dimensional shape of the outline, and any other shapes within the main shape you can see. Later you will practise drawing two- and three-dimensional shapes.'

Practical activity

❒ Hold up an object and ask the children what overall three-dimensional shape they think it is, for example, a mug is a cylinder.

❒ Then ask what two-dimensional shape (the contour or outside edge) they see. To do this they have to flatten the object in their mind's eye, and just look at the outline. A mug is roughly a rectangle.

❒ When they have looked at the outline shape of an object, ask them what other shapes they can see within the outline:

- A mug may have an ellipse at the top, or an oval handle
- The three-dimensional shape of a box might be cuboid, the contour a rectangle and you can also see a diamond within the outline
- Screwed-up paper could be spherical but some of the shapes within it could be triangular
- A figure is cylindrical, its two-dimensional shape is rectangular, but the head is oval, and so on.

Background information
It doesn't really matter what children draw, when they learn to see things in terms of their shape they can draw anything – people, buildings, animals, landscapes. These can all be treated in the same way at the outset of the drawing. Becoming aware of the shape or shapes of the subject will help children to 'find a way in' to their drawings. If they think in the language of shape, the drawings they produce are more likely to resemble the reality of the things they have observed.

'The sphere, the cube,
the cylinder are what Cézanne
called the basic forms,
"all objects can be reduced to these."'
Bert Dobson, Keys to Drawing

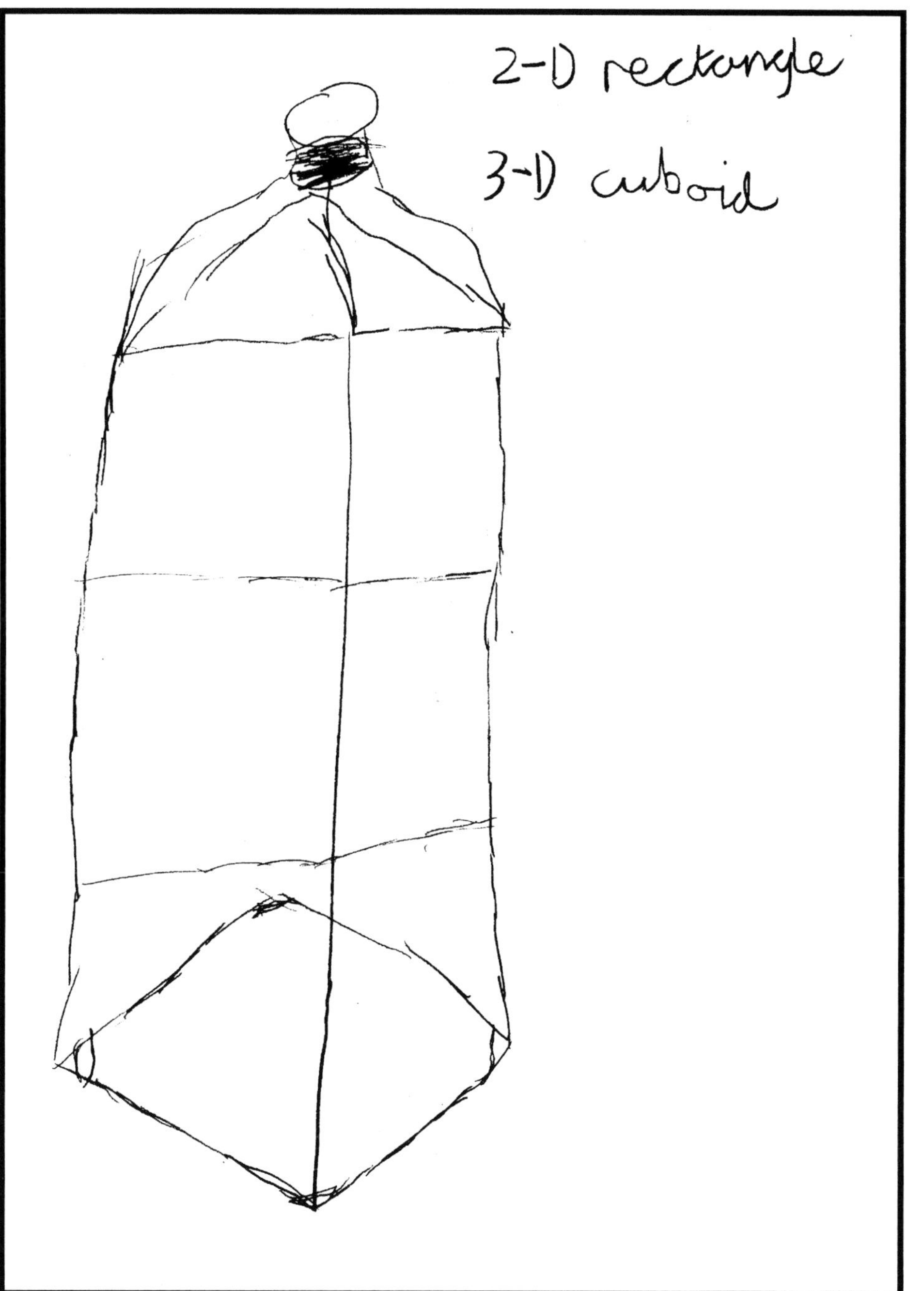

Year 4 child's drawing of juice carton

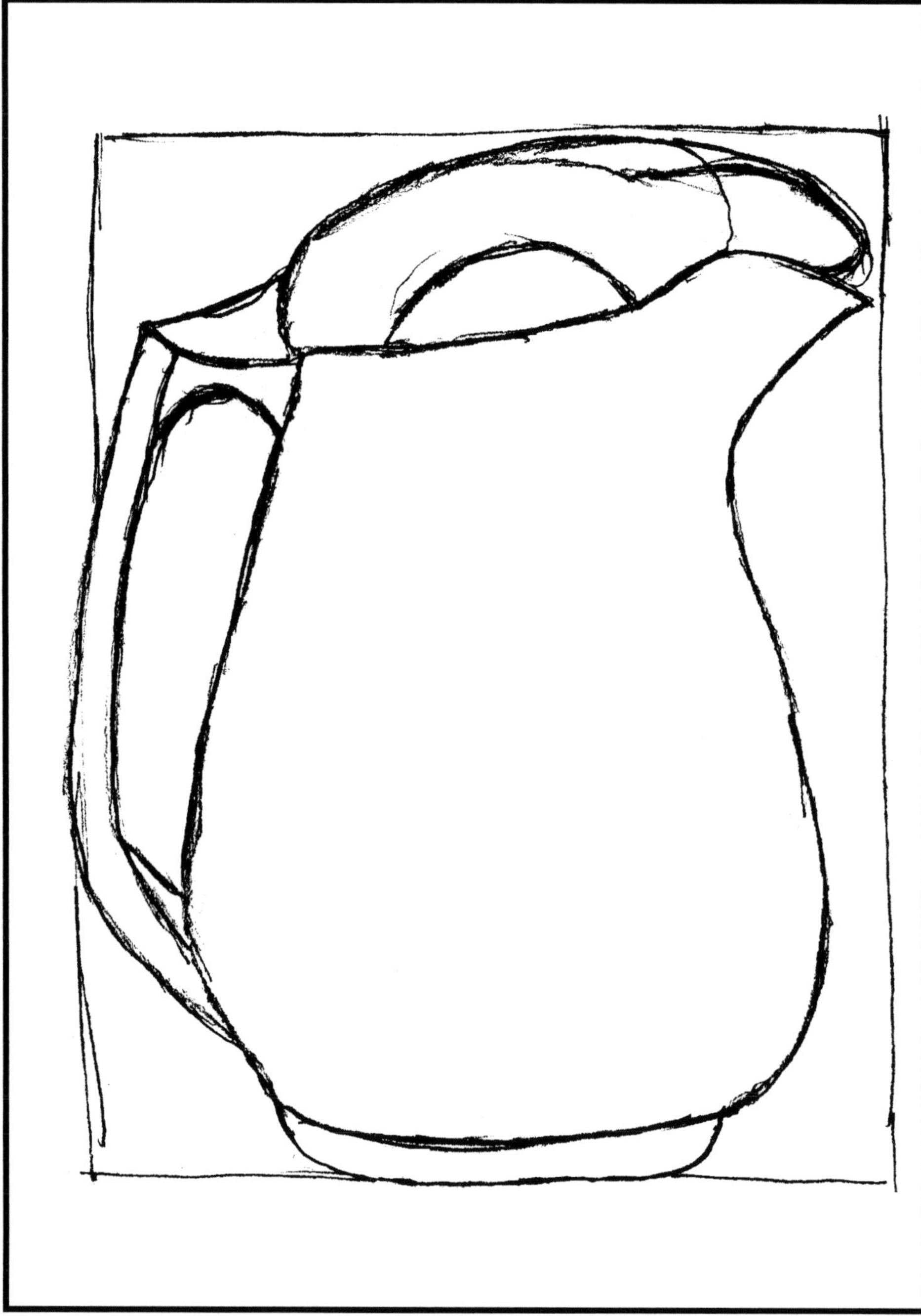

Chris Dennis, Year 4 (drawing of jug showing 2-D rectangle and 3-D cylinder)

USING SKILL

Looking for shapes 2

Time	Resources	National Curriculum
30–45 min.	Sketchbooks B pencils Artefacts that have a fairly obvious overall shape, e.g. table, chair, bottles, mugs, fruit or vegetables, teapots, kettles	1a, 2b, 4a

Introduction

'Drawing shapes is easier than drawing things, and if you can draw shapes you can draw almost anything. Seeing and then drawing the overall shape and then the smaller shapes inside is a really good way to start a drawing. This is what many of the world's greatest artists do. This is what you will be trying out today.'

Practical activity

- ❒ Direct the children's attention to the object they are going to draw.
- ❒ Ask them to identify the outline shape. Suggest they try to flatten it in their mind's eye and look at the main shape they can see.
- ❒ Children draw this shape lightly, filling the page.
- ❒ They now try to identify other shapes they can see within the outline and draw them, e.g. the curve of a label around a bottle.
- ❒ Draw with light lines any shapes outside the main outline, such as the handle on a mug or kettle.
- ❒ Suggest they note where the object is narrowest or widest.
- ❒ Ask if they notice any right angles or parallel or converging lines, such as the sides or legs of a table.
- ❒ As they notice these they should lightly draw them. Once they have the main shapes and angles they can add details, tone and darker lines.
- ❒ They could try to draw as many subjects as time allows.

Background information
This lesson follows on from the skill lesson 'Looking for shapes 1' on pages 78–79. Drawing shapes is much easier than drawing things. Once the overall shape has been identified and drawn lightly, the next steps seem less daunting. Children should think about using the paper sensibly, trying to fit the outline shape onto the paper so it fills the space well. This is an element of composition.

Matthew Tyzak, Year 4

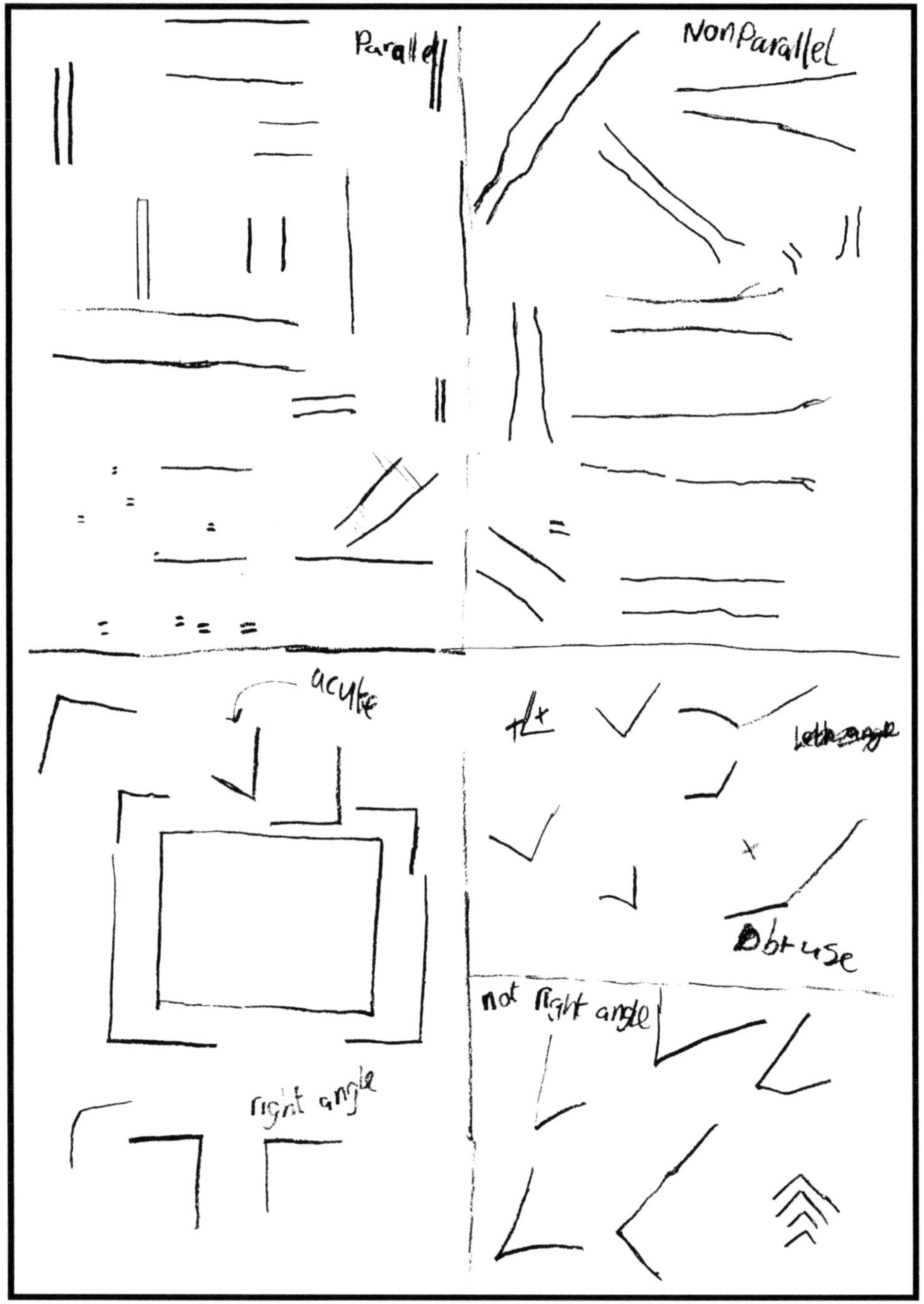

Jordan Prowse, Year 4

Recognizing and drawing right angles and parallel lines

Time	Resources	National Curriculum
30 min.	Sketchbooks Any pencils Some square shapes to draw around (could use set-squares or protractors)	4a

Introduction

'You are going to be drawing and learning to recognize different angles today. This is one of the most useful skills you can acquire. It will help you to check angles in your drawings.

Practical activity

- ❒ Revise what a right angle is. Children can then draw around a square, and then try drawing some lines that meet in a right angle.
- ❒ They then judge by eye if they have been successful. If not, are their angles more or less than right angles?
- ❒ Then they could check with a set-square, protractor or square shape and annotate their drawings.
- ❒ They should practise until they become reasonably competent at drawing and recognizing a right angle every time.
- ❒ Next try drawing pairs of parallel lines by eye (no rulers). Can they judge if they are successful at drawing parallel lines?
- ❒ Draw pairs of non-parallel lines. Compare the two sets.

Background information

This activity needs to be done only if children have not recently covered right angles and parallel lines in maths. It is very useful for them to be able to recognize a right angle and to judge whether another angle is more or less than it. It is equally useful for children to be able to recognize if lines are parallel or not and, if not, what angle they are to each other – opening up or converging. This ability is very important when children are judging how and where a drawing is going wrong. The ability to compare relationships between lengths, widths and angles is a key skill in drawing. That skill is covered in a separate lesson. However, children cannot make comparisons unless they can recognize angles.

Drawing geometric shapes

Time	**Resources**	**National Curriculum**
30–45 min.	Any pencils Sketchbooks and/or copies of Resource sheet 13 (page 141) Lots of two-dimensional mathematical shapes for children to draw round	4a

Practical activities

Circles and ovals

- ❒ Children draw round a small circle, then using a light free line go over the circle a few times.
- ❒ Without the two-dimensional shape, practise drawing circles lightly and freely on the same page. Children should aim to draw very lightly with a flowing motion (teacher could model this) and try to join the circle so the line meets back at the starting point smoothly. This is easier when done quickly rather than slowly and hesitantly.
- ❒ Repeat this activity with an oval.

Squares and rectangles (discourage use of rulers)

- ❒ It helps if children can recognize and draw right angles and parallel lines (see previous lesson).
- ❒ Children draw round a square shape, looking at the angles of the corners, noting that the sides are parallel and equal.
- ❒ Next, without the two-dimensional shape, practise drawing squares, using light lines – judging by eye if they have been successful.
- ❒ Use the same sequence with rectangles.

Cuboids and cylinders

- ❒ Follow Resource sheet 13, or any maths schemes or formulae the school may have for drawing cubes and other three-dimensional shapes.
- ❒ Children may have their own formulae for drawing three-dimensional shapes and might like to demonstrate these on the board.

Year 4 child's drawing of geometric shapes

Background information

Many artists think that, if you are able to draw a sphere, a cube and a cylinder, you should be able to draw anything. Three-dimensional shapes can be quite tricky to draw. Explain that it is just a knack and it can easily be picked up with a bit of practice. It is better that they do not use rulers but rather develop their ability to draw reasonably straight lines by hand.

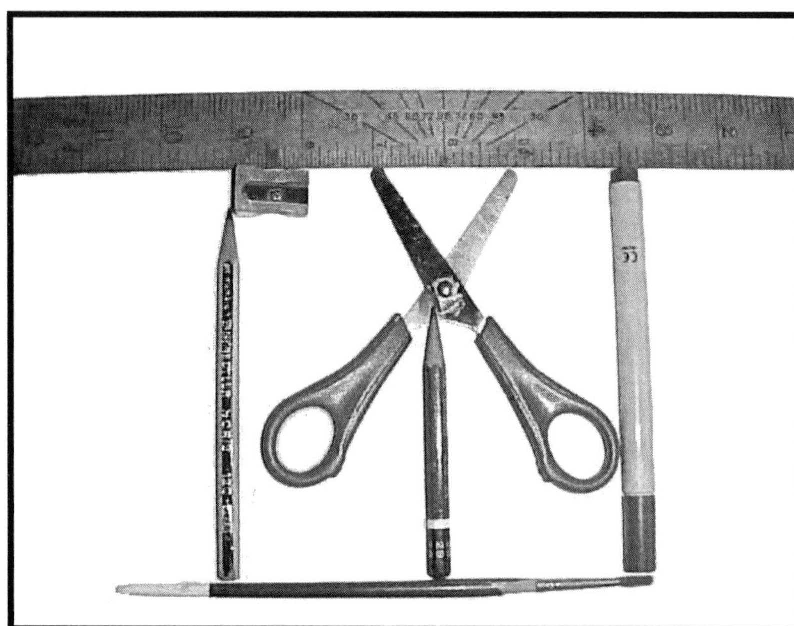

Possible arrangement of objects

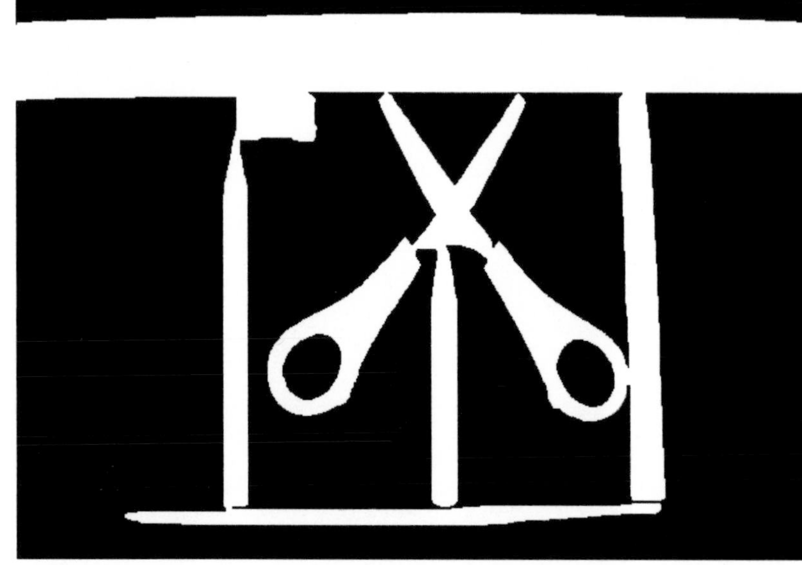

Negative shapes around objects shown in photograph above

Seeing negative shapes

Time	Resources	National Curriculum
15 min.	For each pair of children, a small collection of objects such as scissors, pencils, eraser, book, ruler	4a

Introduction

'The spaces between and around objects are just as important as the objects themselves. Objects take up a space and there is space all around them. These shapes are called negative shapes. Today you are going to start to see those shapes as shapes in their own right. Try to be aware of them from now on when you are drawing. It is another way to help you improve your drawings.'

Practical activity

- Children put a few objects on their desks in front of them in a small group, quite close together. Some could be overlapping.
- Now ask them to look at the spaces between the items, to stare at them for a few moments until they can see them as shapes.
- Explain this is quite hard at first, but it becomes easier.
- They should not try to name the shapes, but try to see them as clearly as the shapes of the items themselves.
- Children then re-arrange the objects and look at the new negative shapes formed.
- Explain that artists are always very aware of these negative shapes when they are composing a picture; they are a very important element.
- Lastly, put a chair up on a table where all the children can see it and ask them to see if they can see any negative spaces between the legs or around the back. This could be done with other large objects.

Background information

The ability to see negative or trapped shapes is an enormous help to children when drawing. They can use these shapes as another way of checking to see if their drawings are reasonably accurate in terms of shape and proportion. First, they need to be able to see them as shapes in their own right and as important elements of the whole subject and drawing.

Seeing and drawing negative shapes

Time	Resources	National Curriculum
30–45 min.	Sketchbooks Sharp B or 2B pencils Resource sheet 14 (page 142) Tracing paper Subject that has clear negative shapes, e.g. large house plant or chair with slatted back	1a, 4a

Introduction

'You have been looking for and recognizing negative shapes. Today you are going to draw them. You should try to concentrate on the negative rather than the positive shapes.'

Practical activity

- ❒ Give out copies of Resource sheet 14, which shows the drawing of a cheese plant.
- ❒ Children lay the tracing paper over and trace through the negative shapes only. Shade them in.
- ❒ Point out how, by drawing just the negative shapes, the object is drawn as well. This should help them to understand that both sets of shapes are important.
- ❒ Next place the object(s) to be drawn on a table or wherever it can be seen.
- ❒ Point out one or two of the negative shapes.
- ❒ Allow plenty of time for the children to look at them before they start to draw.
- ❒ When children start drawing, emphasize drawing the negative shapes only and not to worry about the whole object. (They may only manage part of it anyway.)
- ❒ At the end of the lesson they could shade any negative shapes, so they stand out.

Heidi Green, Year 4 (see page 142 for enlarged version, also appears on front cover)

Background information

The spaces in, around and between objects are generally referred to as the negative shapes. Children often ignore them when drawing, but they are as important as the shapes themselves. They are an important element in composition and children can use them to check the accuracy of the shapes and proportions in their drawings. This should be stressed or they may not take the activity seriously.

Sighting

Using a pencil to check angles

Time	Resources	National Curriculum
10 min. or less	Any full-length pencils	4a

Introduction

'Today you are going to learn a technique that will help you to check the different angles in whatever you are drawing. Artists use this technique to make judgements about the relative angles and sizes of things. This technique is called sighting. You are going to just check angles today. That means how the angle of one thing compares with another. When you are drawing you need to make lots of little checks as you go along.'

Position required for sighting

Practical activity

Children could use the classroom as a subject, or any object that is more than an arm's length away.

Tell the children to:

- ❒ Hold a pencil out vertically in front of them with their arm fully extended (elbow locked). They should wrap their fingers around the pencil and hold their thumb up on the side facing them.
- ❒ Close one eye and line the pencil up with any vertical edge.
- ❒ Now find other vertical edges.
- ❒ Then keeping their pencil at the same vertical angle, find edges of shapes that are at slightly different angles to their pencils.
- ❒ They should repeat this, but with their pencils held out horizontally, looking for horizontal edges and then edges that are at slightly different angles.
- ❒ They will think this is a little silly at first but if they use sighting to check angles when they are drawing they will soon realize it is a very useful strategy.

Background information

Sighting is a very useful skill as it helps children see relationships between angles. *Is this bit roughly horizontal? Have I got it horizontal in my drawing? Is this at the same angle as that?* It is a way of checking how accurate their drawings are, and for detecting where something may have gone wrong. Knowing what has gone wrong and what they are going to do about it gives children more control over their drawings. It only works when the subject being drawn is more then an arm's length away. Sighting can also be used to compare lengths and breadths of lines and shapes.

Drawing using sighting

Time	Resources	National Curriculum
35–40 min.	Sketchbooks B pencils	1a, 1b, 4a

This lesson should ideally be done straight after the skill lesson 'Sighting' on the previous page. Revise the technique if some time has elapsed.

Introduction

'You have learned about sighting and how it helps you to check the angles in your drawings. Today you are going to draw the part of the classroom you can see from where you are sitting, using sighting to check if you have got the angles about right.'

Practical activity

- ❒ Ask children to look around the room without sighting.
- ❒ Ask them to look for any vertical edges or lines they can see: sides of bookcases, doors, tables, whatever is in their field of vision.
- ❒ Ask them to make a mental note of the horizontal edges, tabletops, chairs, windows, etc.
- ❒ Next children use sighting to check if the edges they thought were vertical actually are vertical.
- ❒ Then they check the horizontal edges in the same way.
- ❒ Next they find some edges that are neither vertical nor horizontal.
- ❒ They try to judge how far from the vertical or horizontal they are, by comparing them against the vertically or horizontally held pencil.
- ❒ Children now sketch the view, using light lines (main shapes no details).
- ❒ Say you will be expecting to see them using sighting to check the angles in the room against the angles they have drawn.
- ❒ Once they are satisfied that the main angles in their drawings are reasonably accurate they should carry on with their drawings, adding a little tone and detail.

Potential pitfall!

There tends to be a degree of silliness when children first use sighting. This quickly wears off as they use the skill and see how useful it is.

Hannah Clark, Year 4 (drawing of interior of classroom, including ceiling angles and window at the far end of the room)

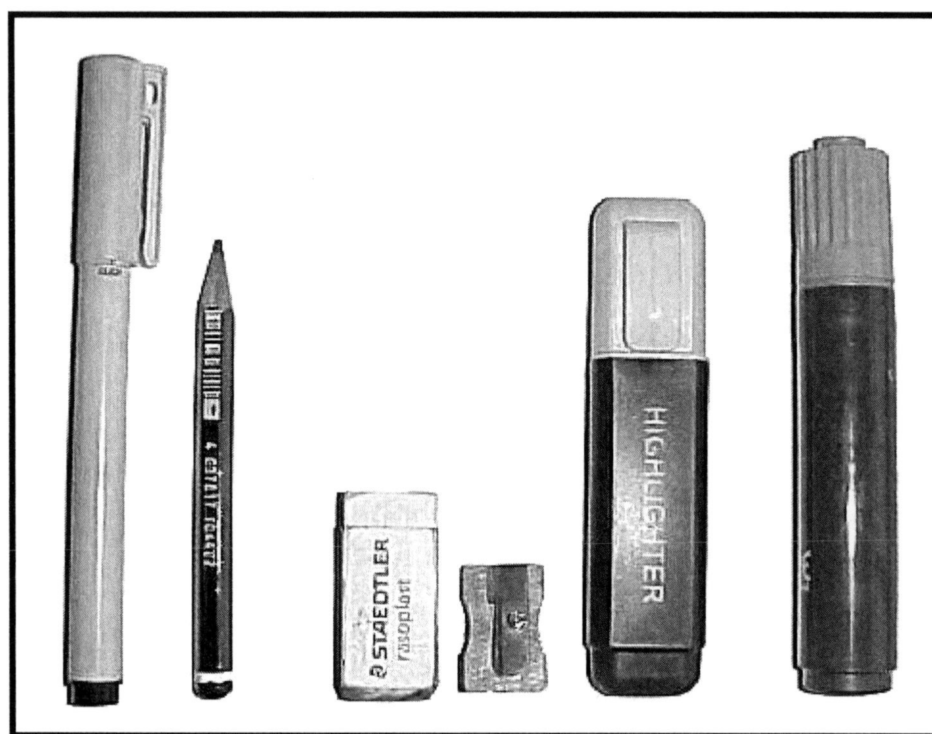

Example of a collection of small objects of varying heights and widths

Learning to see relationships between line and shape

Time	Resources	National Curriculum
20 min.	Collection of small objects such as, pens, pencils, books, erasers, ruler, scissors, pencil sharpener (per child)	4a

Introduction

'You are going to learn to spot the differences in sizes of objects. You will be talking to yourself in your head, asking yourself questions and looking for the answers. It will help you improve your drawing, because it will give you a way of checking if you have the shapes and sizes of things about right.'

Practical activity

- ❒ Children arrange a few objects in front of them on the table.
- ❒ Children look at an object and compare length to width.
- ❒ Ask them to judge with their eyes what the difference is, twice as long, more or less than twice as long?
- ❒ Now ask the same questions about another object in the arrangement. Tell them just to think about it.
- ❒ Now choose a third object. Ask them to compare it with the first two.
- ❒ Model some questions they could ask. For example:
  - ✳ How long is it compared to ...?
  - ✳ Is it longer? Twice as long? Shorter?
  - ✳ How thick is it?
  - ✳ Which is the thickest part?
  - ✳ How much thicker/thinner/wider/narrower is it than ...?
- ❒ They could ask the questions with a partner.
- ❒ They should now look at the arrangements of objects and ask the same kinds of questions of one object compared to another (see examples on the following page).
- ❒ Explain that this is the kind of internal dialogue that should be going on during drawing.

> 'Exercise your eyes to see the length and breadth of things.'
> *Leonardo da Vinci, Treatise on Painting*

Possible questions

- ❐ How much longer is the felt tip than the pencil?
- ❐ Twice as long? Less than twice as long?
- ❐ Which is thicker, the highlighter pen or the pencil?
- ❐ Is the thick felt tip longer than the pencil?
- ❐ Which is longer? By about how much?
- ❐ How wide is the eraser compared to the pencil sharpener?
- ❐ Is the pencil closer to the felt tip or the eraser?
- ❐ Is the space between the pencil and the felt tip the same as between the pencil sharpener and the highlighter pen? Which is wider?
- ❐ Is the highlighter pen lined up with the pencil, felt tip, pencil sharpener and eraser?
- ❐ Which is closest to / furthest from the pencil sharpener?
- ❐ Is the width of the highlighter pen similar to the length of the eraser or the pencil sharpener?

Children could make up their own similar questions.

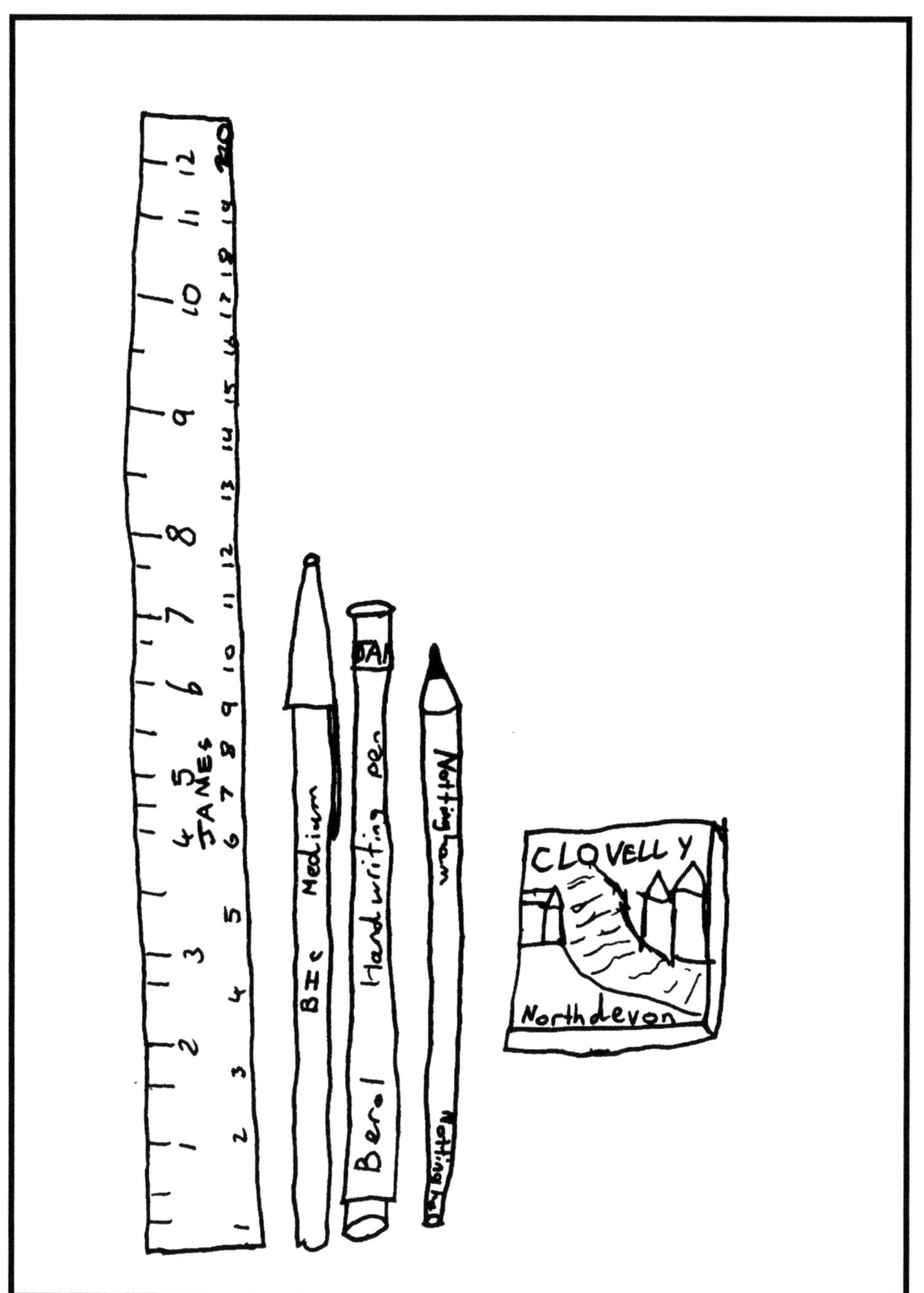

James Chapman, Year 4 (drawn after looking to see relationships between line and shape)

Background information
This skill will help children perceive differences in proportions of their subjects. If they do not see that one thing or part of a thing is wider, longer, shorter than another part, they will not draw it that way. They will tend to draw what they think is there. This is one of the most difficult habits to break in children's drawing. Directing their looking is a vital step in improving their drawing. This is also the beginning of developing internal dialogue that should go on while children are drawing.

'Reading with Globe' by Michael Craig-Martin (a photocopiable version appears on page 143). Reproduced with permission from Tate, London 2005

Seeing relationships between line and shape when drawing

Time	**Resources**	**National Curriculum**
30–40 min.	Sketchbooks B pencils Collection of objects: books, pencils, scissors (per child) or a still life collection of objects (per group of children) If needed, copies of still life pictures or Resource sheet 15 (page 143)	1a, 1b, 4a

This could be an opportunity to introduce 'still life'. Show Resource sheet 15, or other examples.

Introduction

'You have been learning the skill of judging the comparative length and width of objects, and the spaces between them. You can use this skill when drawing larger-scale subjects such as landscapes or interiors. You ask yourselves the same kind of questions: How wide is this wall compared to that wall. How much taller is this building/tree/hill than that one? How much wider are the windows than the door? Don't forget to look at the spaces between things as they are just as important. Whatever the subject matter, you should be asking these questions while you are drawing. You can ask them again as your drawing progresses. Look at your drawing to see if you have got the proportions about right. If not, have another look at the subject, try to work out where you went wrong, check one measurement against another. Then alter the drawing straight away. Never put in detail or shading until you are happy that you have the main shapes about right.'

Practical activity

- ❒ Before starting to draw, children take a good long look at the subject, comparing the lengths and widths.
- ❒ They think about these before making any marks on the paper.
- ❒ When drawing a symmetrical object such as a bottle or jug, they could draw a light line down the middle of it. This will help them to judge if they have drawn both sides the same.
- ❒ Children should:
  - ✳ Use light lines and not put in any detail or tones until the main bones of the drawing are fairly accurate
  - ✳ Keep looking backwards and forwards between their drawing and the subject, checking relationships between objects, and asking themselves the kind of questions suggested on page 89 (these could be written on the board)
  - ✳ Look at the spaces between objects and compare distances
  - ✳ Check if one object is in front of another, and if part of the object behind is hidden
  - ✳ Spend roughly half their time looking and half drawing.

Year 4 child's still life drawing of different sized objects, arranged closely and overlapping

Looking and drawing from different viewpoints

Time	Resources	National Curriculum
30 min.	Sketchbooks B or 2B pencils A child's bicycle	1a, 4a

Introduction

'Today you are going to be drawing this bicycle, but you will be drawing it upside down. You will need to look very carefully before you start to draw. You should look for the overall shape, and then what other shapes you can see. Check to find the highest and widest parts, and look carefully at the way the main shapes are connected. Don't worry about details like the writing or the spokes to begin with. Try to think about the shapes, spaces, lines and angles you can see.'

Practical activity

- ❒ Balance the bike upside down on its handlebars.
- ❒ Children should:
  - ✻ Think about how they will fit it onto the paper and to make a few preliminary marks to indicate roughly where the top, bottom and sides will be
  - ✻ Use light lines until they are sure the main proportions are roughly accurate
  - ✻ Spend roughly half their time looking and half drawing.
- ❒ When they have been drawing for five minutes or so, stop them and ask them to check if they have drawn the wheels the same size or the same height.
- ❒ Then ask them to take a look at their drawings and then check the bike and then look back at their drawings again.
- ❒ They know that the wheels touch the ground at the same point so they tend to draw them level, although when a bike is upside down the wheels might be at different heights. Wheels are often different sizes on children's bikes: ask them to check the relative sizes of the wheels against what they have drawn.
- ❒ They should also check the distance between the two wheels in their drawings and on the bike. These are key places where they can go wrong.
- ❒ Tell them to alter anything that needs changing before adding any detail.

Potential pitfall!

Children often get hooked on drawing the writing and logos on a bike, failing to notice that the proportions of the bike in their drawing are way out. Discourage any drawing of detail at the early stages of the activity.

Background information

Looking and drawing from different viewpoints will help children draw what they see rather than what they think they can see. This works particularly well with an artefact that they are very familiar with. The purpose of the lesson is to demonstrate how they should always try to look with fresh eyes and to forget what they know about something. Children unintentionally refuse to see the true shapes and sizes of things because they have preconceived ideas about them. This is a good example of the left side of the brain causing problems in drawing. There is more about this on pages 70–71. Children might like to hear a little about it.

Year 3 children's drawings of a bicycle that has been placed upside down

Looking strategies you could use when drawing

1. Looking for the main shapes.
2. Looking for shapes within shapes.
3. Looking for parallel lines.
4. Looking for right angles.
5. Looking for negative shapes.
6. Sighting to check angles.
7. Looking at comparative lengths and widths.

Name ________________

Date ________________

Self-assessment of looking strategies

Did you use any of these strategies when you were drawing?

- ❒ Looking for the main shapes .... Yes / No
- ❒ Looking for shapes within shapes .... Yes / No
- ❒ Looking for parallel lines .... Yes / No
- ❒ Looking for right angles .... Yes / No
- ❒ Looking for negative shapes .... Yes / No
- ❒ Sighting to check angles .... Yes / No
- ❒ Looking at comparative lengths and widths .... Yes / No
- ❒ Using light lines at the start of the drawing .... Yes / No
- ❒ Which strategies helped the most? (put the numbers)

- ❒ Do you need to go over any of them again .... Yes / No
- ❒ Which ones?

- ❒ What would you like to get better at in drawing?

Year 4 child's 10 minute portrait of headteacher standing on a chair

Figures and faces

Year 3 child's pencil portrait showing use of face divisions

Rationale

One of the most important aspects of school life is the adults and children who make up the school community. Therefore what could be more useful or relevant to children in drawing than to be able to draw people?

Drawing people (figure drawing) is a fundamental part of art education. Children are quite likely to be asked to include people in illustrations across the curriculum. That probably means being able to do it from memory. They need to be able to draw figures with fairly accurate proportions, quickly and easily. To do this they need to be taught a few basic rules, and they need practice.

Drawing people is like drawing anything else in so much as you need to look hard at the subject. However, it is more obvious when the drawing doesn't go well, as we all know what people look like.

In this chapter children will cover some of the basic rules of figure drawing. Both year groups will draw from life and from memory. They will study both head, and whole-body portraits. They will evaluate their drawings and identify what they might change in their work.

Depicting the human form is the drawing skill that children will use most in primary school.

Common pitfalls

There are some inaccuracies that crop up almost universally when children draw faces and figures:

- ❐ Heads tend to be too big
- ❐ Eyes are too near the top of the head
- ❐ Necks are missing
- ❐ Shoulders are too narrow
- ❐ Arms are too short and with younger children they stick straight out to the sides
- ❐ Feet are too small
- ❐ Both feet point the same way, or
- ❐ Feet are at a 180-degree angle to each other.

In this chapter children will be given strategies to deal with these tendencies, and some tips to make it easier to put things right for themselves.

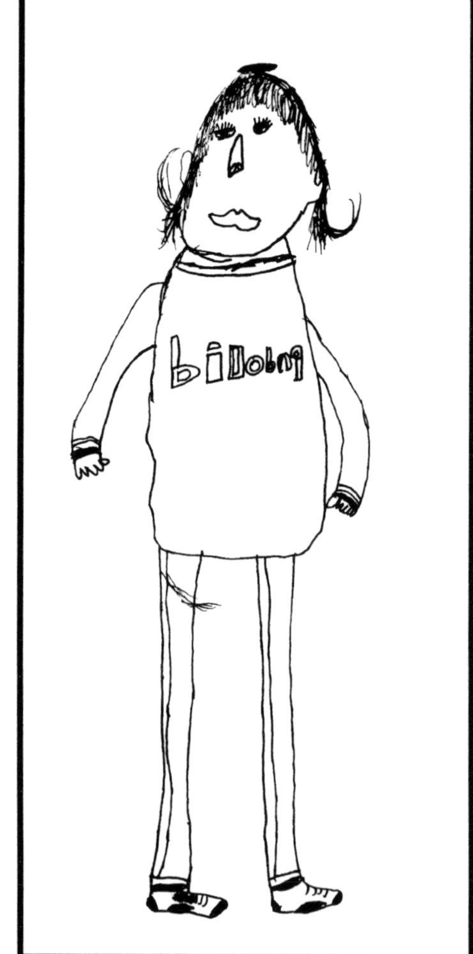

Good example of common pitfalls

Shapes and proportions

These are only intended as a starting point, not a formula. Photocopiable versions appear on Resource sheets 16 and 17 (pages 144–145).

Figure drawing

- ❒ You can fit about 5–6 heads into a child's body (6–7 into an adult's body).
- ❒ The middle of the body is the hip line (not the waist).
- ❒ Arms (when hanging down) end half way down the thighs.
- ❒ The shoulders are at least twice the width of the face.
- ❒ Necks are slightly narrower than heads.
- ❒ Foot length is similar to head length.

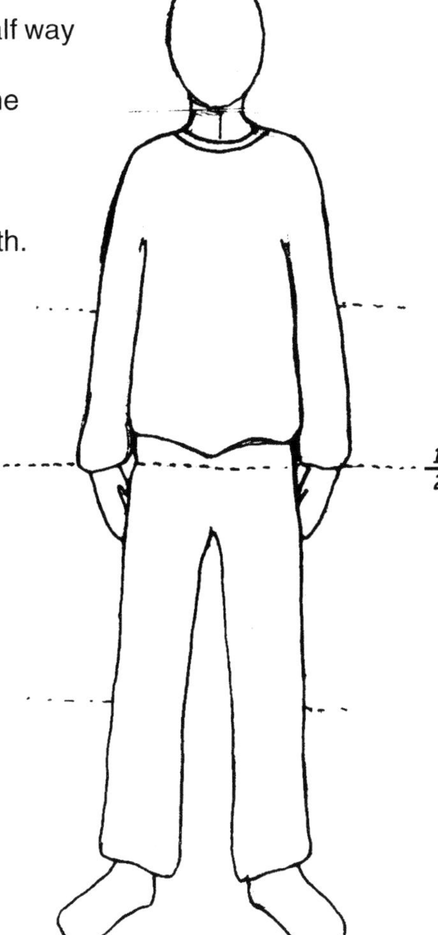

Facial portraits

- ❒ From the front, heads are roughly oval.
- ❒ Faces vary in shape, some are more square, some more pointed, some more rounded.
- ❒ Eyes are almond shaped.
- ❒ Eyelashes grow out of eyelids.
- ❒ Eyes come half way down the face.
- ❒ The pupils are in line with the corners of the mouth.
- ❒ The base of the nose is half way between the eyes and the chin.
- ❒ The mouth is roughly half way between the base of the nose and the chin.
- ❒ You can rarely see the whole iris.
- ❒ The line between the lips is the darkest.
- ❒ Tops of ears are roughly level with eyebrows.
- ❒ Hairline starts below the top of the head (unless the model is balding!).

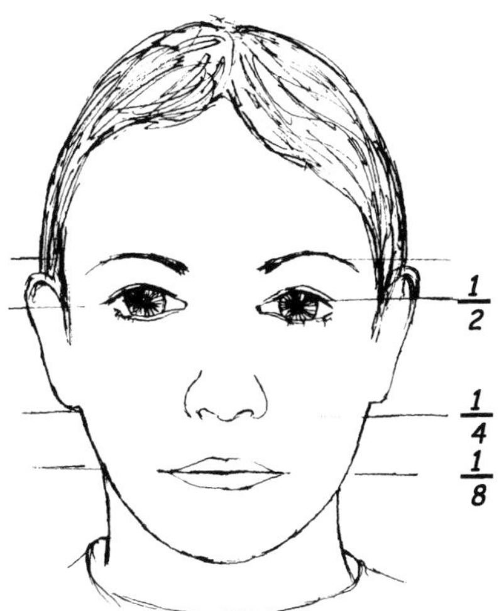

About this chapter

When children reach lower Key Stage 2 they tend to abandon narrative and symbolic drawing and become more concerned with realism. This chapter supports their quest for more realistic figure drawing through a variety of approaches.

In this chapter children will:

- ❒ Be given guidelines and a framework for drawing faces and bodies
- ❒ Draw active poses from life and from memory
- ❒ Develop an awareness of outline and internal shapes
- ❒ Study individual facial features in detail
- ❒ Use mirrors to draw self-portraits
- ❒ Use all these skills to complete a longer pose.

They will evaluate their drawings and identify what they might change in future work.

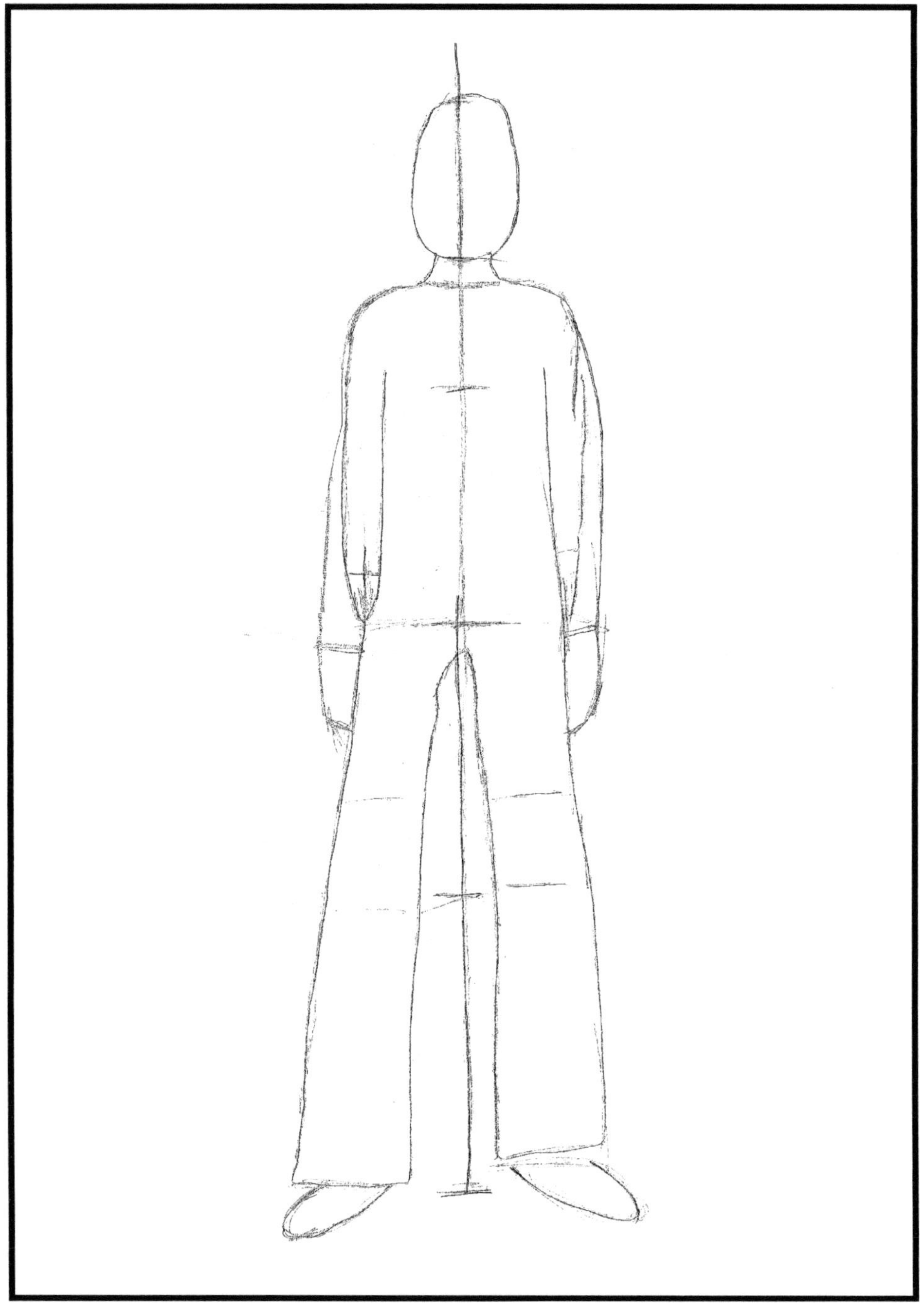

Year 4 child's figure showing body proportion divisions and adjustment of arm lengths

Drawing the whole body

A simple standing pose

Time	Resources	National Curriculum
30 min.	Sketchbooks B pencils Resource sheet 16 (page 144)	1a, 1b, 3a, 3b

Introduction

'Today you will be drawing the head and body; artists call this figure or life drawing.'

Practical activity

- ❐ Go through the main points described on Resource sheet 16, explaining body proportions.
- ❐ Give each child a copy of the proportion guidelines to keep by them as they work. These could be stuck into sketchbooks for later reference.
- ❐ Set up a simple standing pose with arms by the side. Explain that they have 10 minutes to draw the whole figure from head to feet, but no facial features and no details of clothes.
- ❐ Stress the use of light lines in the initial stage of the drawing.
- ❐ Children draw a light vertical line down the page, lightly mark the halfway point, then mark the quarter points. Halve the top quarter.
- ❐ They draw the head as a light oval which takes up the top eighth of the line (the head will be slightly bigger if the model is a child).
- ❐ Explain that the base of the line will be for the feet and remind them that the halfway mark is the hip line not the waist.
- ❐ Children draw the neck, then the shoulders (twice as wide as the head). Next the body, continuing down to the legs.
- ❐ Draw the arms; the hands will come half way between hip and knees.
- ❐ Once they have this framework they can add the rest of the figure, feet and clothes.
- ❐ Ask them to think about how they will improve in their next drawing.
- ❐ Repeat the activity as often as you have time for.

Potential pitfall!
Children tend to get sidetracked into drawing facial features in detail. These should not be drawn until the body proportions are mapped out fairly well. Otherwise they may have a beautifully drawn face with no time left to draw the body, or a body shape that is way out of proportion and they now have no time to fix it.

Year 3 child's 10 minute portrait showing body proportion divisions

Background information
Children should not draw any facial features or detail on clothes. The focus is the whole-body shape and proportions. Remind them to use very light lines. Explain that they may want to change something. If they have drawn dark lines it will be very hard to make changes.

The teacher could be the model – that way no child misses this initial lesson. It is quite useful to be able to watch them drawing and note how often they look at you. It should be 50% looking and 50% drawing. The pose should be standing, with arms by the sides.

This lesson needs to be done quite often. Their figure drawing skills will improve greatly with practice.

Drawing different poses

Time	Resources	National Curriculum
40 min.	Sketchbooks Any drawing media (charcoal is good for quick sketches, 2B or B pencils for more detailed studies) Resource sheet 16 (page 144)	1a, 1b, 3a, 3b 5a

To add variety to figure drawing, it is useful to give the children the stimulus of drawing different poses. Models could be different pupils for each pose, unless an adult can be persuaded. Allow 10 minutes for each pose. Do as many different poses as you have time for.

Practical activity

- Set up a standing pose initially; it will be easier for the children to remember and check body proportions.
- Remind children of the basic rules of these.
- As in the previous lesson, draw a line first and mark off the head, body and legs.
- Start drawing from the head, leaving out facial features. Check how many heads they can fit into the body (should be about 6 or 7) and adjust head size if necessary.
- When main body proportions are fairly accurate, suggest adding features, detail and some tones and textures.
- Use the model breaks for evaluation. Ask the children to think about how they will improve and develop their next drawings.
- In subsequent poses, try different arm and leg positions. Try poses with a prop, for example, pushing a broom or one foot raised on a football.
- The same guidelines of proportions apply but as some limbs will be at angles, children could start to look for shapes within the pose to help them judge sizes.

Potential pitfall!

Seated poses can be quite challenging because of foreshortening.

Year 4 children's pencil and charcoal drawings of different poses

Year 3 child's figure drawing, drawn without looking at the paper

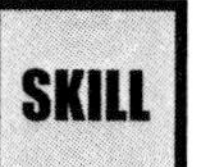

Contour figure drawing

Slowly drawing the outline of the figure without looking at the paper

Time	Resources	National Curriculum
30 min.	Sketchbooks B or 2B pencils	1a, 1c, 2b, 4a

Introduction

'Today you are going to try out a new drawing technique. It is called contour drawing. Your drawings will not look like figures to begin with, but you will be getting better at looking very closely and drawing only what you see.'

Practical activity

- ❒ Set up a simple pose and tell children they are going to draw the figure without looking at the paper and they don't have to worry what the drawing looks like.
- ❒ They need to decide where on the outline of the figure they will start looking and to fix their eyes on that point.
- ❒ Explain that as their eyes travel very slowly around the outside of the figure their pencil must draw equally as slowly, drawing exactly what their eyes see at exactly the same time. It is as if the eyes give a message directly to the pencil.
- ❒ Children should try not to take the pencil off the paper, and resist the temptation to look at their drawings.
- ❒ Explain that the slower the eyes travel the easier it is to draw.
- ❒ As this type of drawing requires intense concentration, restrict each pose to five minutes.
- ❒ When a few contour drawings have been completed, they can begin to glance down at the paper occasionally during the next drawings to briefly check their progress and add a few internal lines.

Potential pitfall!
Initially children may find this activity hard to take seriously. They will find their drawings hilarious. Some children will rush the drawing and really what they will be doing is drawing a figure from memory, rather than by looking.

Year 4 child's figure drawing, drawn without looking at the paper

Background information
Pure contour drawings are done without looking down at the paper. The drawing medium moves over the paper at the same rate as the eyes travel over the subject. It is as if the drawing appears on the paper by itself. This is an exercise in intensive looking. It will need to be explained carefully to the children and they will find it rather strange at first. Drawings may only take a few moments, or several minutes.

Year 4 child's pencil drawings completed in 2 minutes from an active pose

Gesture figure drawing

Time	Resources	National Curriculum
30 min.	Sketchbooks 4B pencils, graphite, Conté crayons (soft pastels) or charcoal (any drawing medium suitable for fast, flowing drawing)	1a, 1c, 2b, 4a

All the poses should be very active: throwing a ball, bending down to tie a shoelace, reaching up, etc. Sketching could be done of a PE lesson, in the playground, of animals or small children.

Introduction

'The drawings you will be doing today are called gesture drawings. These drawings try to catch the feeling of the pose, what the model is doing, rather than how they actually look. The drawings are done very quickly, less than a minute each. Try to use a continuous line, without taking the pencil off the paper. Artists often have to record what they see quickly before the scene changes. It is a very useful skill to develop.'

Practical activity

- ❐ Set up an active pose which children must complete in one minute.
- ❐ Do as many different poses as you have time for.
- ❐ Allow one minute to draw the figure.
- ❐ Children should try not to take their pencil off the paper whilst drawing.
- ❐ Remind them to keep what they know about body proportions, size of head and length of limbs in the back of their mind whilst drawing.

Figure drawing from memory
Seeing the figure as a whole shape

Time	Resources	National Curriculum
30 min.	Sketchbooks 4B pencils, graphite, Conté crayons (soft pastels) or charcoal (any drawing medium suitable for fast, flowing drawing)	1a, 1c, 2c

Introduction

'You will be doing some very quick poses today, drawing the model from memory. You will have a few moments to look at the pose, and then you will have to quickly draw what you have seen. Try to see the figure as a whole shape; this is the best way to start a life drawing.'

Practical activity

- ❒ Ask the model (it could be you) to take a pose and hold it for about half a minute. During this time describe how the model is posing, e.g. arms are crossed, head is slightly to one side.
- ❒ Tell the children that the most important piece of equipment they have for drawing is their eyes; ask them to pretend they are like a camera. They need to take in the whole thing, creating a mental snapshot.
- ❒ Then the model steps down and the children have a few minutes to draw what they remember.
- ❒ Repeat this activity with different poses each time.

Background information
When drawing completely from memory children need to remember the whole figure, the overall shape and mood of the pose. Most drawing, with the exception of contour drawing, involves some memory. When children are looking back and forth between the model and the paper, what they are doing is memorizing little bits at a time. This exercise is good training as it helps them to see the figure as a whole shape.

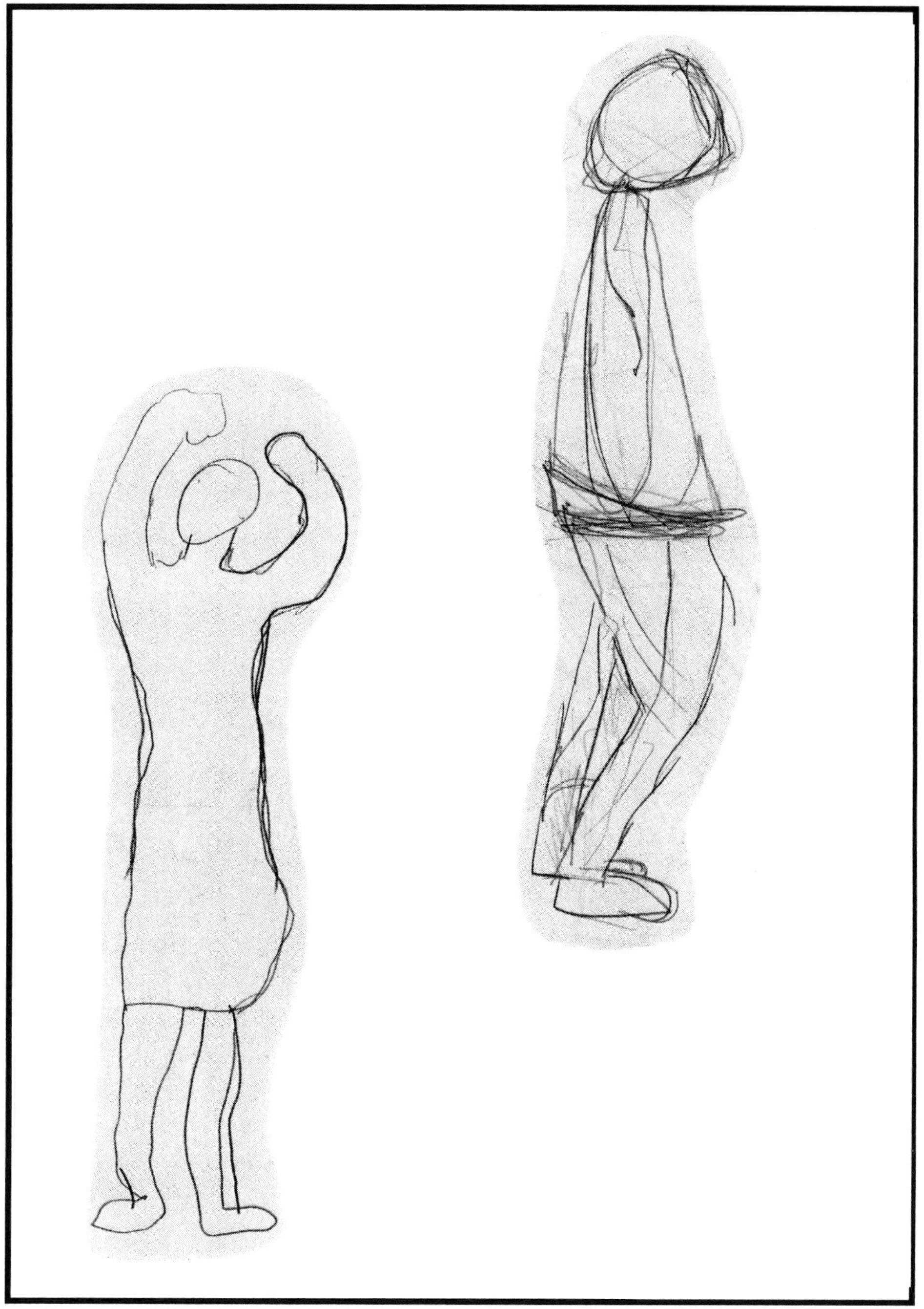

Year 3 child's 3 minute drawings from memory

Year 3 child's drawing showing divisions marking position of features

Drawing heads and position of features

Time	Resources	National Curriculum
30 min.	Sketchbooks B or 2B pencil Mirrors Resource sheet 17 (page 145) – optional	1a, 1c, 4a, 5a

Introduction

'Today you are going to draw heads and faces. You will be looking at where the features are on the face and looking carefully to see how the hair grows.'

Practical activity

- ❒ Talk about head shape first; explain that although head and face shapes vary from person to person, they are mostly oval. Say, *'Think rugby ball, not football.'*
- ❒ Children now draw a large oval lightly, filling the paper.
- ❒ They draw a halfway line lightly across the face.
- ❒ Using mirrors, the children look at their eyes and draw eyes on this line (one eye-width apart).
- ❒ Draw eyebrows above. Ask them to look at the shape of their eyebrows as they vary considerably.
- ❒ Draw a line half way between the eyes and the chin. Explain that this is roughly where the nose ends.
- ❒ Ask them to look at the shape of their nostrils and draw in that part of the nose along that line.
- ❒ Draw the mouth half way between the nostrils and the chin.
- ❒ Draw ears (tops in line with eyebrows, lobes in line with mouth).
- ❒ Using a child as an example, point out that the hairline starts *below* the top of the head. Ask them to look at which way their own hair grows: down the forehead in a fringe, combed to one side or back. How far down the side of the head does it come? Does it cover the ears?
- ❒ Then draw in the hair.

Background information
Children tend to make similar inaccuracies when drawing heads and faces. Eyes are often drawn too high up the face. This could be because they consider the eyes to be the most important facial feature, so they draw them near the top of the head. Necks tend to be too narrow and the hairline starts too high up the head.

Daisy Burt, Year 4

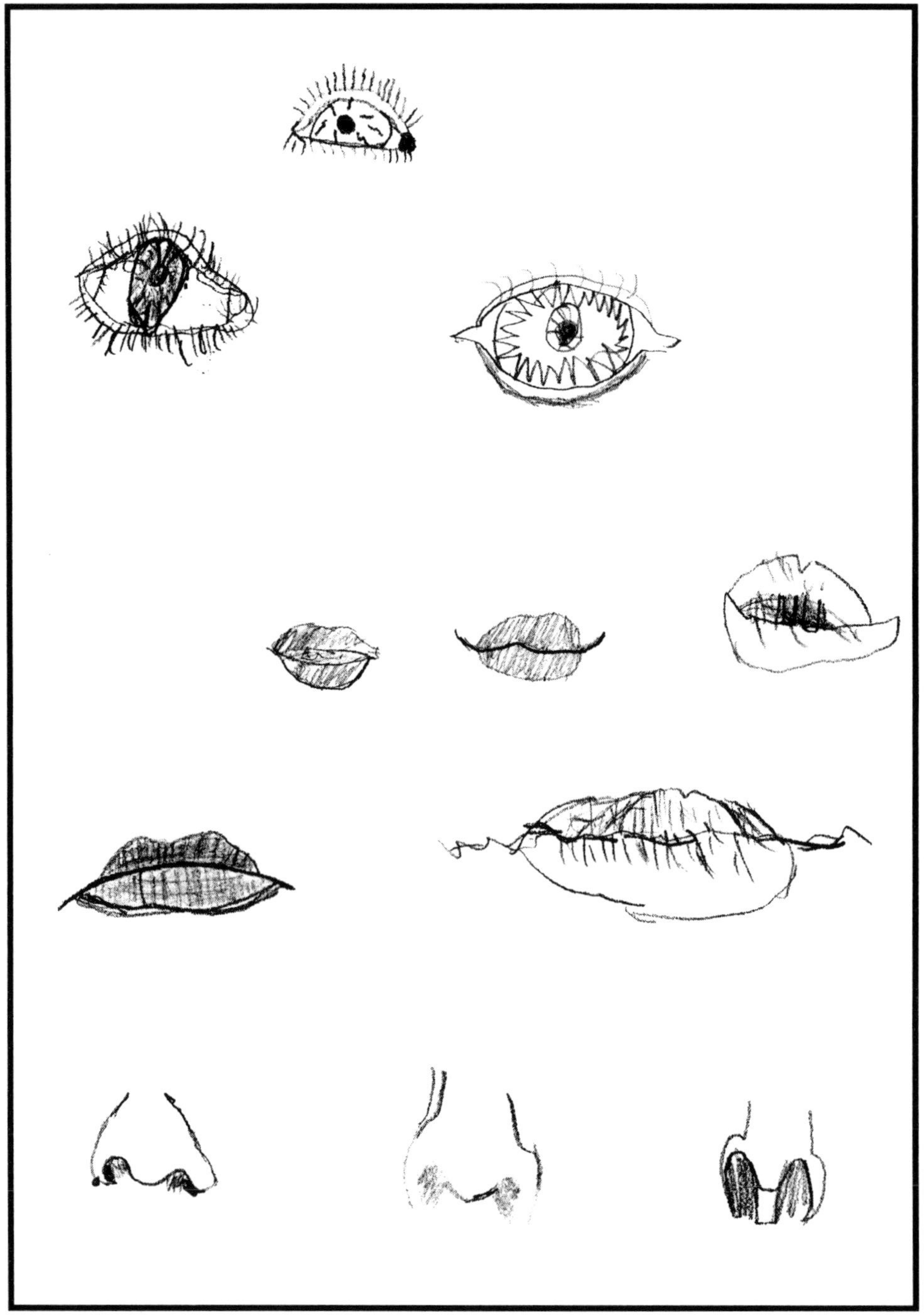

Year 4 children's pencil drawings of features

Drawing eyes, mouths and noses

Time	**Resources**	**National Curriculum**
45 min. approx.	Sketchbooks B or 2B pencils Mirrors	1a, 1b, 2b, 5a

Introduction

'Having worked on head shapes and the positions of the features, you are going to spend more time looking at and drawing eyes, mouths and noses.'

Practical activity

- ❒ Using mirrors, children look at the shape and colour of their eyes and eyelashes, comparing them with a partner's.
- ❒ Point out that you cannot see the whole of the iris; the top and bottom are generally hidden by the eyelids.
- ❒ Now ask them to look at where their eyelashes grow from, and the angle from the eyelid (to the side rather than upwards), and how they often grow in little clusters on the lower lid.
- ❒ Next look carefully at the iris and notice the lines radiating from the pupil and the dot of reflected light near the middle.
- ❒ Children draw their eyes, remembering to include all the things they have noticed.
- ❒ Repeat this looking activity with mouth shapes.
- ❒ Explain that as the line between the lips is the darkest children should draw this first. Then lightly draw the upper and lower lip line.
- ❒ The top lip is often in shade and so is darker than the lower lip. Children lightly shade the top lip.
- ❒ Noses are quite difficult. Suggest drawing the shadows rather than the nose itself – the hollows of the nostrils and the shadows either side and beneath.

Background information

Children tend to have developed schema for drawing eyes and mouths. This lesson encourages them to have another look at the shapes and draw what they see rather than what they think they know about them. Profiles are more difficult than full-face portraits and could be left until upper Key Stage 2.

Drawing faces

Time	Resources	National Curriculum
30–40 min.	Sketchbooks B pencils Mirrors Resource sheet 17 (page 145) – optional	1a, 5a

Introduction

'Today you are going to draw self-portraits. You are going to draw just faces not the whole body. This is an opportunity for you to apply all that you have learned about drawing features and about their shapes and position. You could try to create a likeness to yourself. You will have about 20–25 minutes to complete the drawing.'

Practical activity

- ❒ Remind the children of the aspects of portraits that they have covered so far: the oval head shape, the position and shapes of features.
- ❒ Children lightly draw an oval shape for the head, filling the paper so there is plenty of room to draw the features.
- ❒ Draw a light line to mark the halfway point, and another to divide the lower half equally.
- ❒ Then draw the neck, noting how wide it is and how it curves out as it joins the shoulders.
- ❒ Before continuing children should look carefully in the mirror at the shape of their faces to judge the overall shape and alter the oval to match their own face shape more closely.
- ❒ Now draw the features, using different types of line, tones and textures, with continual reference to the mirror.
- ❒ Before adding the hair, look to see where it grows from, how far down the face it comes, if it covers the neck, if it is wavy or straight, if the ears are visible.
- ❒ Lastly they could add details such as freckles and moles.

Key reminders

- ❒ You can rarely see the whole iris.
- ❒ Eye sockets are often shadowed; there are upper and lower eyelids.

Thomas Gatehouse, Year 4

- ❒ The line between the lips is the darkest.
- ❒ The upper lip is often in shadow.
- ❒ There are vertical hollows above the top lip and on the sides of the nose.
- ❒ Use different types of line, tones and textures.

Background information
This is an opportunity for the children to apply all that they have learned about drawing features and about their shapes and position. They can try to create a likeness of themselves using line, tone and texture.

Full portrait

Long pose

Time	Resources	National Curriculum
40–60 min.	Sketchbooks Any B pencils (B–4B) Someone to pose Resource sheet 16 (page 144)	1a, 1b, 3a, 3b 5a

As this is an extended pose, it would be better if the model is not one of the class. Model's breaks can be used for the children to check their work and consider their next steps.

Introduction

'Today you are going to do a full portrait. You will have at least half an hour, excluding the model's breaks, to draw the whole figure. That means you will have plenty of time to check the proportions of the figure and make any necessary changes before you add any details. The finished drawing should include tone, texture and any patterns you see.'

Practical activity

- ❒ Revise guidelines for shapes and proportions.
- ❒ Set up a relaxed standing pose, one the model can hold for 8–10 minutes at a time.
- ❒ Suggest that children try to see the figure as a whole shape, and plan how it will fit on the paper.
- ❒ Revise the system for mapping out body and head proportions covered in the key skill lessons (pages 98–101).
- ❒ When the framework is mapped out, they should be able to do a light drawing of the whole figure, starting with the head.
- ❒ Discourage any drawing of facial features or hair at this stage.
- ❒ Once children are satisfied that the proportions are fairly accurate they can go ahead and add details. This is a good moment to draw their attention to folds and textures in clothing, shadows and patterns.
- ❒ Lastly add features and hair.
- ❒ Children should consider their success against the pointers they were given, and consider what changes they would make next time.

Charlotte Rice, Year 3

Chalk and charcoal

Year 3 child's chalk and charcoal drawing

Alex Lyons-Martin, Year 4

Rationale

Chalk and charcoal are excellent drawing media as they encourage children to think about a whole subject and not to become lost in detail, as they often do. For example, they will carefully draw eyelashes when they have not yet drawn the whole figure, they will start to draw patterns on clothing before they have checked body proportions.

Chalk and charcoal encourage them to think big, to concentrate on main features and to think about lights and darks from the moment they put their first marks on paper.

Drawing with chalk and charcoal will help children to get into the habit of seeing and thinking in tones, rather than detail and colour. It can be free, messy and dramatic, or controlled, delicate and subtle. It is also relatively easy to create pleasing pictures and so helps to boost confidence and self-esteem.

Chalk and charcoal are classic drawing media. Across the ages artists have used these drawing materials, for example Rembrandt, Whistler and the contemporary American artist Jim Dine.

Media knowledge

Charcoal is made by sophisticated methods nowadays, but it is basically just burned wood and is the oldest drawing medium. It has been in use since early cave people covered the walls of their caves with drawings of the animals they hunted, using burned sticks from their fires and charred bones. It has been made for centuries by the controlled and partial burning of wood. It makes bold black marks, which can be smudged, blended and lightened in different ways.

Chalk is often used with charcoal as a way of picking out highlights and for mixing with charcoal to create mid tones. Adding chalk highlights can bring a charcoal drawing to life, giving it contrast and sparkle.

Different types of charcoal
Stick charcoal
The commonest types of charcoal are vine and willow charcoal, which are made in different thicknesses and with different degrees of hardness. Medium thickness is the most versatile, although the fine is useful for more delicate work and the thick for drawings covering large areas or dense coverage. Children tend to worry about charcoal breaking so it is a good idea to snap it into approximately 4 cm lengths in advance.

Charcoal pencils

These are a less messy way of using charcoal as the children's fingers hold the wooden shaft not the actual charcoal, and broken pieces are not forever dropping on the floor. However, they need constant sharpening so can be more trouble than they are worth.

Compressed charcoal

These small sticks are made from powdered charcoal compressed with a binding material. They do not break as easily as stick charcoal but they are less easy to dust off.

Chalk

Ordinary blackboard chalk is perfectly adequate. White chalk pastels or Conté crayons (soft pastels) could also be used.

Fixing drawings

All soft media like chalk and charcoal need 'fixing' as these materials are so soft they will continue to smudge and fade if not fixed when the drawing is finished. Special fixative can be purchased from art suppliers but cheap unscented hairspray makes an acceptable alternative. The drawings should be sprayed when children are out of the room.

Year 3 child's chalk and charcoal cube (cube outline drawn by adult)

Tips and techniques

To avoid smudging during drawing

One of the characteristics of chalk and charcoal is that they smudge. Drawings can be spoiled by being leaned on as work progresses so provide the children with pieces of scrap paper to lay between their hands and the drawing. Their hands will rest on this and not on their drawing.

Papers

Chalk and charcoal work looks best on mid-tone tinted sugar paper such as grey, buff or brown. Charcoal is sympathetic to the texture of paper allowing the grain to show through, so paper with a slight roughness to it is ideal. Very smooth or shiny paper should be avoided as the charcoal will slide on the surface and lose its density.

Blending

To create an expanse of blended tone, first build up an area of scribbled marks, pressing evenly but not too heavily. Use the tip of a finger to rub the surface lightly to blend the marks together. The finished effect is a soft deep shadow which can be drawn over or made deeper by repeating the process. Chalk and charcoal can be blended in the same way.

Lightening

Charcoal can be lifted or lightened in different ways: a soft eraser, pieces of cloth, tissues or even pellets of soft bread. If erasers are being used they need to be as soft as possible, and kept just for use with charcoal, as cleaning them after will take time. Some old erasers could be cut into quarters, as children do not need a whole eraser each.

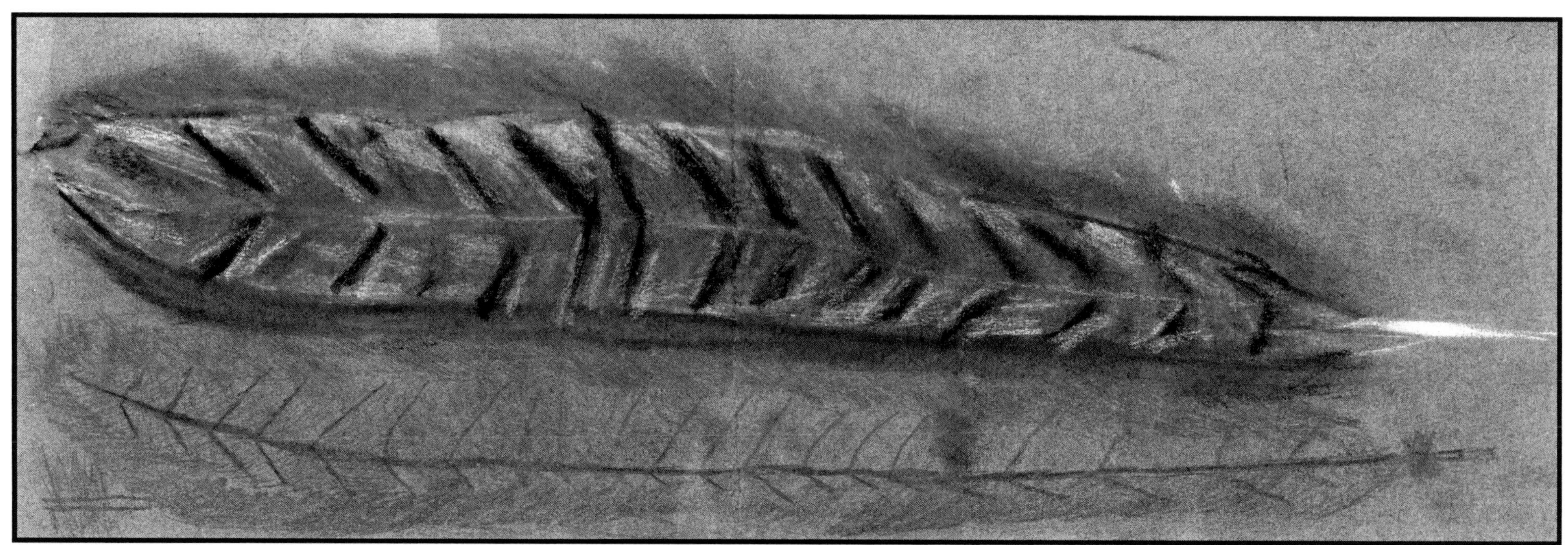

Jade Tanton, Year 3 (see colour example on front cover)

Charcoal wash
A brush dipped in water applied to parts or the whole of a charcoal drawing creates a grey wash. The tones of the wash soften the fierceness of the black lines and when the wash is dry it can be drawn over, creating a layered effect.

Keeping clean
Children should cover their clothes and roll up or push back their sleeves. They can become agitated at the state of their hands during a charcoal lesson. Explain that some aspects of art are messy and that's the way it is. Discourage washing hands during the lesson; they should just dust their hands together to get the worst off, and carry on.

About this chapter

Children can create dramatic and pleasing effects using chalk and charcoal.

They are ideal media for capturing spectacular scenes, for example an urban landscape, bare winter trees, a sudden fall of snow, or a stormy sky with lashing rain.

Chalk and charcoal can also be used to great effect in portrait work. The chalk highlights 'lift' the drawings, giving them a sparkle and crispness. Children are often delighted with the results.

In this chapter children will experiment with making marks with chalk and charcoal. They will blend and smudge them together and use chalk to create simple highlights. They will look carefully to identify the darkest and lightest tones in their subject and try to recreate these in chalk, charcoal, or a blend of the two.

Joshua Lee, Year 4

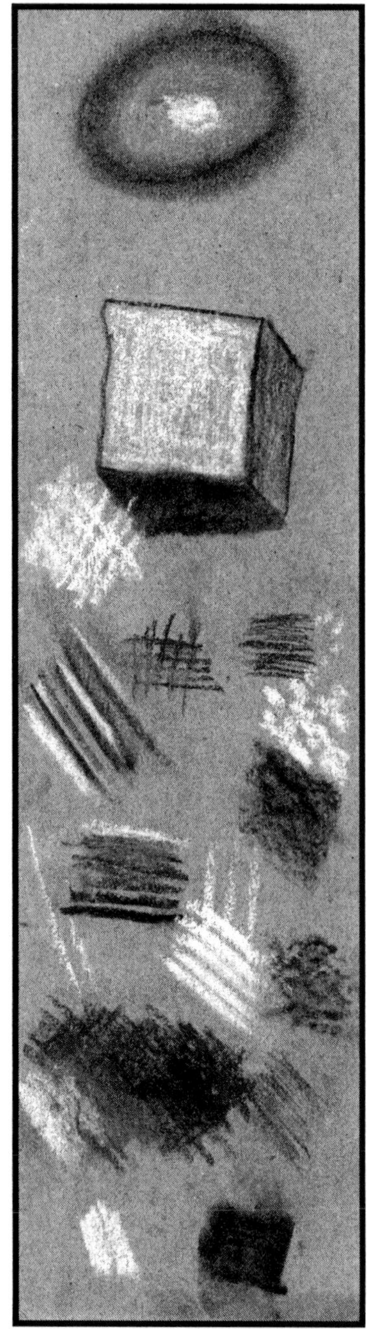

Year 4 children's recordings of marks in chalk and charcoal

Making different marks with chalk and charcoal

Time:	Resources	National Curriculum
15–20 min.	Mid-tone sugar paper (any colour, but grey and brown look good) Charcoal, medium thickness (broken into 4 cm lengths) White chalks or white soft chalky pastels Fixative (see Glossary) Scrap paper Large piece of paper for teacher modelling	2a, 2b, 4a

Introduction

'Today you are going to investigate different effects you can make with charcoal, and you are going to use chalk to blend with the charcoal to make highlights.'

Practical activity

❒ Children make a range of different marks, using the side as well as the point of the charcoal.
❒ Tell them to smudge some of the marks.
❒ Do they do the same with the chalk and experiment with blending the two.
❒ Draw some cubes on their paper while they are doing this (see page 34).
❒ Ask them to shade in one side very darkly, one side a medium tone and one side white.
❒ Children draw a circle and blend the tones around the circle with a fingertip, getting lighter as they get nearer the middle. Add a chalk highlight in the middle.
❒ Model this and show the three-dimensional effect this creates.

Background information

To make sure that work is not spoiled by being leaned on and smudged as work progresses, provide the children with a piece of scrap paper that can be laid over any completed sections of their work. Snap the charcoal into 4 cm lengths approximately; it won't break so readily and it will enable them to make marks using the side as well as the point of the charcoal. Spray work with fixative at the end of the lesson, when children have left the room.

Drawing with chalk and charcoal

Time	Resources	National Curriculum
30–40 min.	Mid-tone sugar paper Charcoal, medium thickness (broken into 4 cm lengths) White chalk or white chalky pastels Child to model or feathers, shells or any artefacts (natural or man-made) that include a good range of tones and some very light areas (see list on page 69) Fixative (see Glossary) Scrap paper	1a, 2a, 2b, 4a, 5a

If there is not time to collect a range of artefacts, portraits are good subjects. Choose a child to model whose appearance includes a range of contrasting tones with some very light areas, e.g. shirt collar, black shoes. If you choose cream or buff paper, the base colour will double as a skin tone.

Introduction

'Now you have experimented with the marks you can make with chalk and charcoal, you are going to draw (whatever) *looking carefully at the different tones and noting the lightest and darkest areas. You will need to think about how you will create these using chalk and charcoal. Remember that chalk and charcoal smudge beautifully, so don't forget to smudge them if you want to create a particular effect.'*

Practical activity

- ❒ Children do a quick line drawing of the subject in chalk.
- ❒ Then they start adding the tones, first the darkest areas in charcoal, next the lightest areas using the chalk.
- ❒ They can create the tones in between with either different depths of tone in charcoal, or by blending chalk and charcoal.
- ❒ Chalk and charcoal lines can be added over the tones.
- ❒ Detail, if appropriate, can be added last.

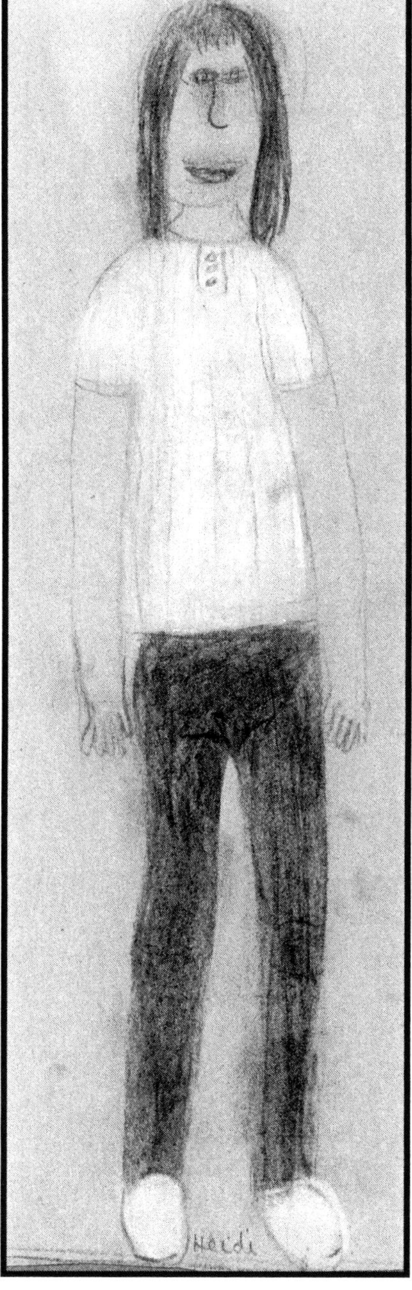

Heidi Green, Year 4 (see colour example on front cover)

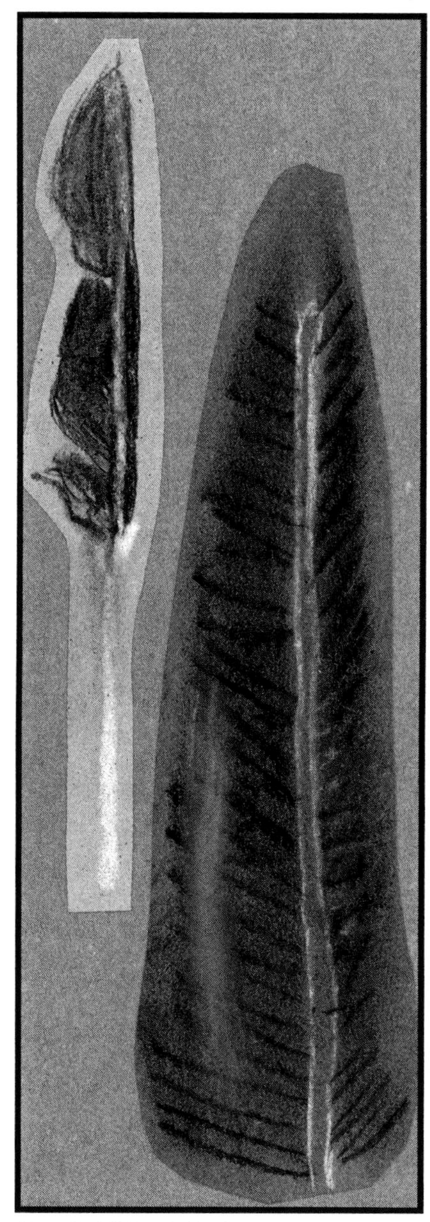

Year 3 children's feathers

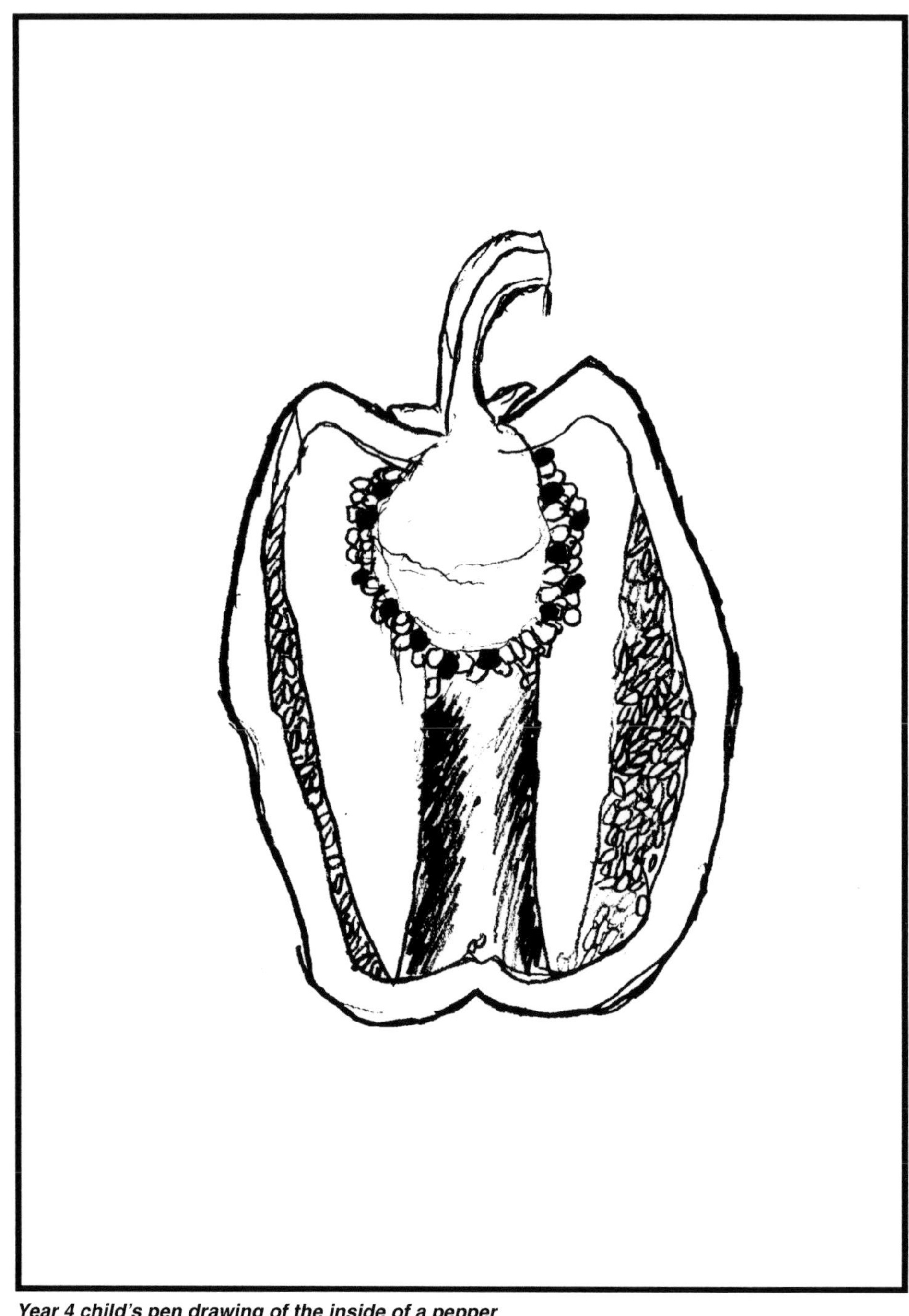

Year 4 child's pen drawing of the inside of a pepper

Evaluation and assessment

Assessment

Children need to reflect on their artwork and should share in assessment where appropriate. They should be clear which aspect of their artwork is being assessed, and what they need to do to meet the assessment criteria.

Realistically, drawing needs only to be assessed in broad terms: identify those children who are struggling and will need to cover the work again or in a different way, and those children who have excelled and could be stretched.

One way might be to broadly group pupils into three ability bands. At the end of a term, chapter or whenever appropriate, select a small number of pupils from each band and assess their work. From this make a general assumption that other pupils in the same band will have achieved a similar standard. At the end of the next term or chapter, select a different group of pupils so that over the course of a term (or a year) all pupils will have been assessed.

Another way to make the assessment process easier is to photocopy the class list and attach it to the drawing skills assessment sheet (Resource sheet 18, page 146). Highlight the aspect(s) you are going to assess. (Limit this to a maximum of three, unless this is an end of year assessment.) Then, using a colour code (e.g. green for excellent, yellow for satisfactory and red for problems), highlight the children's names with the appropriate colours on the class list. Further comments could be added if necessary. An example assessment record is given on this page.

Drawing assessments

Class:

Date:

Colour code
Green = Excellent
Yellow = Satisfactory
Red = Needs further help

1. Uses a variety of lines in drawings
2. Uses tone in drawings
3. Identifies areas for development in own drawings

	1	2	3
John Brown			
Priya Gil			
Mary Green			
An Other			

Example of assessment record

Evaluation and assessment

Assessment should inform planning. If the majority of the class have not met the success criteria, the task needs to be re-evaluated.

Try to be specific when making your judgements:
- ❐ Was it too hard?
- ❐ Was the explanation clear enough?
- ❐ Does it need to be done again in the same way or differently?
- ❐ Which elements of my teaching do I need to change?
- ❐ When and how will this be done in the same way or differently?

Figure and face drawings could be assessed against the shapes and proportions guidelines found on page 97 and Resource sheets 16 and 17 (pages 144–145). Looking strategies can be monitored using photocopies of page 94.

Older or more able children could check their own drawings, write comments on their achievements and give themselves targets, as in this example:

> *'I am pleased with my portrait. I think I managed to get the head about the right size. I think the legs are a bit too short and next time I will draw the feet bigger.*
>
> Shane, age 8

It is as well to support them with their targets, otherwise they tend to be vague or nearly impossible. For example, *'I want to get better at lines,'* or *'I want to be able to draw dinosaurs fighting to the death.'*

Using success criteria to evaluate children's work

Success criteria should really be drawn up with the pupils as the direct teaching or explanation is taking place. For example, after the skill has been taught but before it is going to be used in a context, say, *'We have been learning how to make our drawings more interesting by using lots of different lines. I want you to remember to use as many of the different kinds of lines as you think will be right for the job in your drawings today* (run over the variety of lines covered). *I shall be looking at your drawings to see if you have used a range of lines.'*

Use a 'must, should, could' system of success criteria. For example, for a Year 3–4 lesson on line work in pencil, write up on the board:

Success criteria
1. You **must** use a good variety of different lines.
2. You **should** use both the side and the point of the pencil.
3. You **could** use lines to create the look of different textures.

Work can then be judged against these criteria. Four criteria are really the maximum.

Success criteria are also useful for children's self-assessment.

There are success criteria for using line in pencil drawings on page 23 in the chapter on Line.

Self-evaluation

In order to evaluate their work, children need to be given the vocabulary necessary to do this and possibly also a framework.

Internal self-evaluation

During the drawing process, a constant internal evaluation should be taking place. Examples of this kind of internal dialogue are on pages 89.

Further self-questioning might include:

- ❒ How is this going?
- ❒ Am I pleased with it?
- ❒ What should I change?
- ❒ How am I going to change it?
- ❒ Is it finished?
- ❒ What is good / not so good about it?
- ❒ How does it look if I hold it away from myself a little?
- ❒ How would it look to someone else?
- ❒ How does it look on the paper?
- ❒ Have I placed it on the paper well?

Spoken self-evaluation

Internal self-evaluation naturally leads on to being able to review what they have done and say what they think and feel about it.

Here the vocabulary may need to be modelled by teacher questioning.

The following questions could be asked:

- ❒ What are you most pleased about with this piece of work?
- ❒ What part do you think is most successful? (the composition, the use of media, the tones, textures, patterns, shapes)
- ❒ What did you find most difficult?
- ❒ What problems did you meet?
- ❒ How did you solve / not solve those problems?
- ❒ If you did it again is there anything you would change?
- ❒ How would you change it?
- ❒ If you had more time what would you do next?
- ❒ Are you proud of it?
- ❒ Would it look very different / better if you ... used different paper/ media / changed the scale / looked at it from a distance / changed the colours?

Developing this kind of questioning will help children talk about their work and be able to make internal independent judgements as they mature.

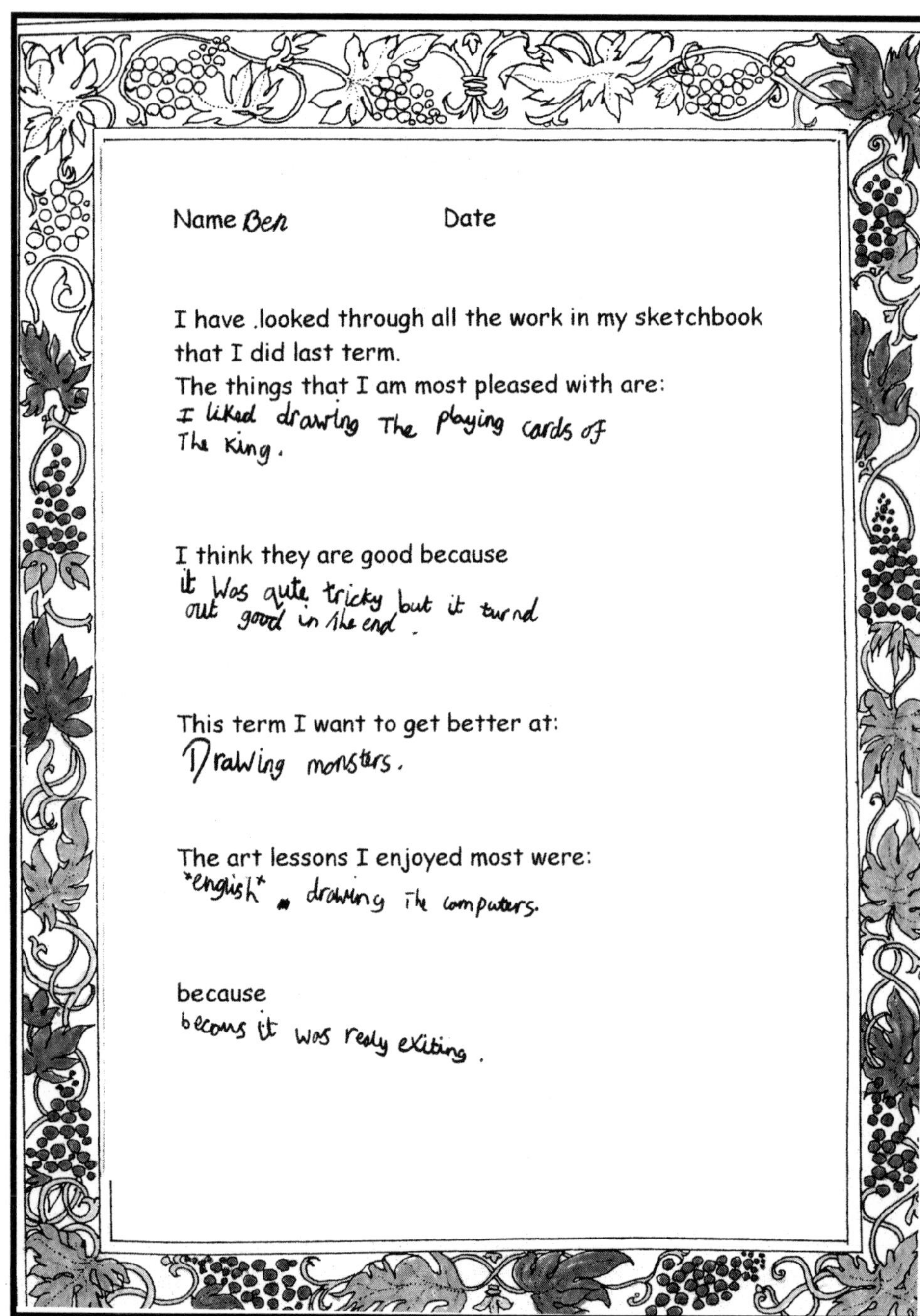
Name Ben Date

I have looked through all the work in my sketchbook that I did last term.
The things that I am most pleased with are:
I liked drawing The playing cards of The King.

I think they are good because
it Was quite tricky but it turnd out good in the end.

This term I want to get better at:
Drawing monsters.

The art lessons I enjoyed most were:
english drawing the computers.

because
becous it was realy exiting.

Example of Resource sheet 19 completed by Ben Burgess-Farrant

Written evaluations

Written evaluations can take different forms.

Children could annotate their work on the border or underneath, especially in their sketchbooks. Language is as for spoken self-evaluations. For example:

> *'I am really pleased with this. I think I made the house look three-dimensional, but I think the trees are too small.'*
>
> Daisy, aged 8

Children could use Resource sheet 19 (page 147) – see the example on this page. These are very useful at the end of a chapter, term or year. They can be pasted into sketchbooks and referred to at a later date. For example, *'Remember what you said you wanted to get better at this term? Look back in your sketchbooks and remind yourself of what you wrote.'* Children could also include personal target, e.g. *'Next term I want to get better at ....'*

The same kind of language can be used when writing comments in sketchbooks. For example, *'This is a careful, sensitive drawing. Were you pleased with it? Which part were you most pleased with?'* Or, *'I can see you had problems with this. What did you find most difficult? How would you do it differently if you did it again?'*

Children could be encouraged to look for teacher comments and questions in their sketchbooks and write a response if appropriate. They could also be encouraged to periodically look back through their sketchbooks to see if they think they are making progress, and write comments against their favourite piece of work. For example: *'I am really proud of this because ....'*

Resource sheet 18 (page 146) provides a comprehensive drawing skills assessment list for individual children.

Peer evaluation

Children should be able to review the artwork of their peers and say what they think and feel about it. The same kind of language can be used for this as for self-evaluation. Children, however, need to learn to be sensitive to each other and to be 'critical friends'. They need to be able to trust each other and be thoughtful and supportive in their comments. In the early stages of developing peer evaluation they need to be confined to positive comments. Later, when trust has been built up and children are better able to express their responses using appropriate vocabulary, some supportive criticism can be introduced. Again this will need to be modelled. For example:

- ❒ What do you think Emma could do to this drawing to make it even better?
- ❒ What problems do you think Dan had with this drawing? How could he solve it?

The peer evaluation can be built into the lesson, and then used in the plenary or summing up at the end of the session. At appropriate points during the drawing lesson, ask children to stop drawing and take a walk around the classroom and have a look at each other's drawings. Tell them to do this in silence with no spoken comments. Ask them to look at each other's drawings and ask themselves questions like:

- ❒ Is it good? What is good about it?
- ❒ Is it not so good? What has gone wrong?
- ❒ How should it be put right?
- ❒ If it was your drawing what would you do next?
- ❒ Are there any good ideas (not copying) you could use in your drawing?

Explain to them that artists get inspiration from other artists. Artists will often talk to each other about their work and the ideas that are generated will often be crucial to the artist's development.

At the end of the lesson one child could be asked to select another pupil's piece of work to comment on. This could be modelled. For example:

- ❒ Why do you like this drawing?
- ❒ What do you think Jade has done particularly well?
- ❒ How do you think she has achieved that effect?
- ❒ Did she remember all the things she was supposed to do (relating to the focus of the lesson)?

Then Jade could be asked:

- ❒ Are you pleased with it?
- ❒ If so, why? What were you most pleased with?
- ❒ Would you change anything it you had time?
- ❒ How would you do it differently next time?

She in turn could be asked to choose another child's work to talk about.

Potential pitfall!
Children often choose their best friend's work to make positive comments about. Pre-empt this by saying you will be asking them to give precise reasons why they think their chosen drawing is good.

Year 4 child's pen drawing with watercolour, inspired by Paul Klee (see colour examples on front cover)

Reporting and tracking progress

One way to keep track of progress is to collect sample drawings from the whole class biannually or termly. These can be annotated and kept in a file. Over a number of years this will give a record of each child's drawing development over their time in school.

Children's drawings tell a lot about children's maturity and something of their character.

The filed drawings are useful for planning and for reporting to parents and showing to Ofsted as evidence of progression.

The drawings must be collected in the same way each time and in the same circumstances. For example, children should be allocated the same time for each sample drawing (e.g. 10 minutes), be given the same medium (e.g. pencil), and the same subject matter (e.g. figure drawing), it will then be easier to compare drawings.

Drawings can be compared against the previous term's drawing and against the general standard of the year group.

Another way would be to take a sample of a figure drawing one term, a landscape the next term and a close observational drawing from the last term. These drawings can be annotated, with specific strengths or weaknesses noted and possible ways forward. The class teacher or the art co-ordinator could keep the files.

Recording coverage of work

To check coverage of chapters, photocopy the relevant part of the contents list. Highlight the lessons covered, possibly making a written note beside the lesson of the programmes of study covered. These are to be found in the box at the top of most lesson pages. The skills in this book cover all the programmes of study relating to drawing, evaluating and developing work.

A colour code could be used: green for covered satisfactorily, and red for lessons that were not successful for some reason. A note could be made by these for future reference.

To check for National Curriculum coverage, photocopy the programmes of study for the appropriate year group and highlight the ones that have been covered.

Both these records of coverage could be kept in a planning or records file.

If you are using the QCA schemes of work, the skills required could be taught prior to delivering the QCA unit. Some QCA units cover a fair amount of portrait work, such as Unit 3a, Portraying Relationships. Other QCA units which involve research and observational drawing would benefit from having drawing and looking skills taught prior to the delivery of the unit.

Reports

Here are some statements which might be useful when writing reports:

- ❒ Has acquired / is acquiring drawing skills after working in a range of media
- ❒ Draws well / is beginning to draw with great sensitivity to line and tone
- ❒ Has developed / is beginning to develop an understanding of pattern/tone/texture
- ❒ Demonstrates good drawing skills in all designing activities
- ❒ Is able to draw and talk about familiar objects
- ❒ Is able to talk about own work using appropriate vocabulary
- ❒ Is able to discuss own work and say what he / she might change or develop in the future
- ❒ Is developing good powers of observation
- ❒ Shows close attention to detail when drawing.

Less positive comments:

- ❒ Finds some aspects of this subject difficult but is working hard to improve skills
- ❒ Needs to be more willing to discuss a piece of work and how it might be improved
- ❒ Must avoid the tendency to rush, and spend a little more time looking and thinking carefully when drawing.

Tara Perham, Year 3 (pen drawing of a harbour viewed from above – see colour version on front cover)

Glossary

Art pastels: Soft chalky pastels, quite smudgy.
Bleed/move: A term which describes what happens when a colour runs when wet or wetted.
Brusho: Powdered watercolour that can be sprinkled directly onto wet drawings, or made up with water as a thin paint. Usually comes in lovely bright colours but can be used for delicate or translucent colour.
Cartridge paper: Slightly rough paper of medium weight, ideal for drawing and painting, can be coloured.
Charcoal: Specially burned twigs used for drawing, comes in different thicknesses. Drawings usually need fixing, with fixative or hairspray.
Composition: The arrangement of elements in a picture.
Conté crayons (soft pastels): Drawing medium made from compressed coloured chalk, often in earth or landscape colours.
Contour: The edge as seen around the outside of a shape or form.
Cross-hatching: Form of shading created by crossed lines.
Elements: As referred to in the National Curriculum for Art and Design: line, tone, shape, form, pattern, colour, texture and space.
Etching: Type of printing, blocks usually made by acid eating into uncovered parts of metal plate. Plate is then inked and prints are taken.
Fixative: Spray used to prevent charcoal or chalky pastel drawings from further smudging. Can be purpose bought, but cheap unscented hairspray makes a good substitute. Fixative should always be used when children have left the room and will not be back for an hour or so, as some children may be sensitive to the fumes.
Foreground: Lower area of drawing representing the area nearest to viewer.
Form: The three-dimensional shape of something.
Graphite: Hard drawing medium, silvery lead colour.
Landscape: Paper alignment when paper is placed with shorter sides vertical.
Medium/media: Different drawing materials: pencil, charcoal, pen, etc.
Move/bleed: A term which describes what happens when a colour runs when wet or wetted.
Narrative drawing: A drawing which tells a story in some way, or a sequence of events.
Oil pastels: Slightly sticky pastels made from coloured chalk bound with oil. Colours blend well. Useful for creating scraper and wax-resist pictures.
Op Art: Short for optical art, pictures usually consisting of lines or shapes that create optical illusions. Often giving the illusion of movement.
Pattern: An image that is repeated in a regular fashion.
People crayons: Commercially produced crayons, usually sold in a pack, made up of colours for different skin hair and eyes.
Portrait: Paper alignment when paper is placed with shorter sides horizontal.
Schema: A formulated drawing that children have arrived at which represents, say, a house, a tree or a person, which they then use every time to represent that subject, even when drawing from first-hand experience.
Single-hatching: A series of single lines, drawn close together to create an area of tone.
Surrealism: An art movement which uses realist images but puts them together in an unusual or dream-like way. Salvador Dali is a Surrealist artist.
Texture: In drawing, texture means creating the impression something has a surface feel to it.
Tone: Darkness or lightness of a colour (including gradual shades of black through to white).
Viewfinder: Piece of black card, plastic or paper with a shape cut out of the middle. This is used to look closely at areas of a drawing or artefact. Can be used as a frame, to help children to compose a picture. The centre shape can be round, oval, square, rectangular, to suit purpose.

Bibliography

Barnes, Rob. *Art, Design and Topic Work 8–13*, Routledge Taylor & Francis
Camp, Jeffrey. *Draw: How to Master the Art*, Dorling Kindersley
Capon, Robin. *Drawing Techniques*, The Crowood Press
Clement, Robert, and Page, Shirley. *Primary Art: Investigating and Making in Art*, Oliver & Boyd
Cole, Roger. *Drawing with Children*, Private publication
Cox, Maureen. *Children's Drawing*, Penguin Books
da Vinci, Leonardo et al. *A Treatise on Painting,* Dover Publications
Devon Curriculum Advice. *Planning, Evaluation and Assessment*, DCA
DfEE. *Art and Design National Curriculum*, Qualifications and Curriculum Authority
Dixon, Peter. *Standing Points*, Private publication
Dobson, Bert. *Keys to Drawing*, A&C Black
Edwards, Betty. *Drawing on the Right Side of the Brain*, Harper Collins
Elderfield, John. *The Drawings of Henri Matisse*, W W Norton
Foster, Patience. *Drawing*, Usbourne
Frank, Frederick. *The Zen of Seeing: Seeing Drawing as Meditation*, Random House
Gormley, Antony. *Drawing*, British Museum Press
Hayes, Colin. *The Complete Guide to Painting and Drawing Techniques and Materials*, Phaidon
Lemos, Pedro. *Applied Art*, Pacific Press Publishing Association
Mann, Ida, and Pirie, Antoinette. *The Science of Seeing*, Pelican Books
Mendelowitz, Daniel M. *Drawing: A Study Guide*, Holt Rinehart & Winston
Nicolaides, Kimon. *The Natural Way to Draw*, Andre Deutsch
Parramon, Joe. *The Complete Book of Drawing*, Phaidon
Robinson, Gillian. *Sketchbooks: Explore and Store*, Hodder Arnold
Sedgewick, Dawn and Fred. *Drawing to Learn*, Hodder Arnold
Simpson, Ian. *Drawing. Seeing and Observation*, A&C Black
van Gogh, Vincent. *The Letters* (translated by Arnold Pomerans), Penguin Classics
Welton, Jude. *Drawing: A Young Artist's Guide*, Dorling Kindersley
Williams, Geoffrey. *African Designs*, Dover Publications

Year 4 child's drawing

Useful websites

www.aboriginalartonline.com
Australian Aboriginal Dreamtime images and stories.

www.accessart.org.uk
Useful information on drawing and children's interactive art activities.

www.artcyclopedia.com
Excellent access to galleries, museums and artists. Easy to search.

www.arteducation.com
Lesson plans on art topics. Includes step-by-step guidance with teacher's notes.

www.artteaching.co.uk
Has links to art galleries. Click on multicultural art for Aboriginal art, Hindu art, Islamic and Ancient Egyptian art.

www.davidmach.com
Website of British artist David Mach.

www.drawingpower.org.uk
Find out about the national campaign for drawing.

www.drumcroon.org.uk
For anyone interested in promoting education through art. Has links to other galleries.

www.google.co.uk
This is a brilliant search engine for images. Having opened up Google, click on 'images' and type in your request. Shows pages of related images.

www.metmuseum.org
Displays more than 3,500 works from New York's Metropolitan Museum, includes growing timeline of international developments in art.

www.moma.org
New York's monumental gallery of modern art.

www.mos.org/leonardo/index.html
Child-friendly site, easy access, lots of interesting information about Leonardo da Vinci. NB: Note his eyes following the cursor on the opening page!

www.nationalgallery.org.uk
The National Gallery website. Has an education section.

www.npg.org.uk
The National Portrait Gallery. An excellent resource, including an education department.

www.nsead.org
Website of the National Society for Education in Art and Design. Among other useful and up-to-date information about art education, has database of around 300 units of work.

www.tate.org.uk
The Tate gallery's website.

www.vangoghgallery.com
Lists and displays all van Gogh's drawings.

Vincent van Gogh, Haystacks near a Farm

(see page 33)

Examples of single-hatching ▼ ▶

'James Leckie and Little Mary' by William Mulready

'And Who Are You?' by Sir Nathaniel Dance-Holland

Example of cross-hatching ▶

'Reaper (e)' by Richard Hamilton © Richard Hamilton 2005. All Rights Reserved, DACS

Paul Klee, They're Biting, 1920, 6

Examples of drawings using line and tone, and just line

'A Seated Boy' by 18th Century British School (a chalk drawing using line and tone)

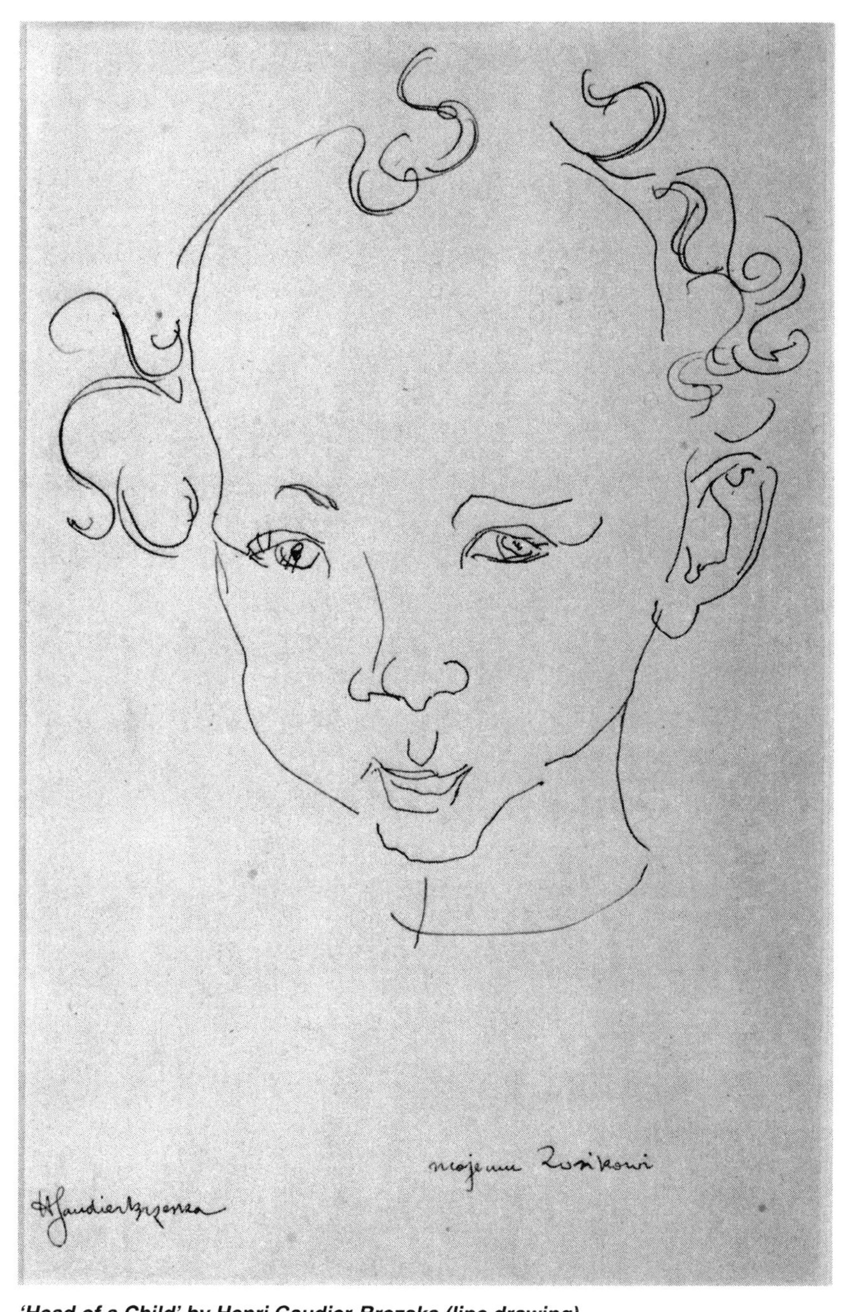

'Head of a Child' by Henri Gaudier-Brezska (line drawing)

(see page 44)

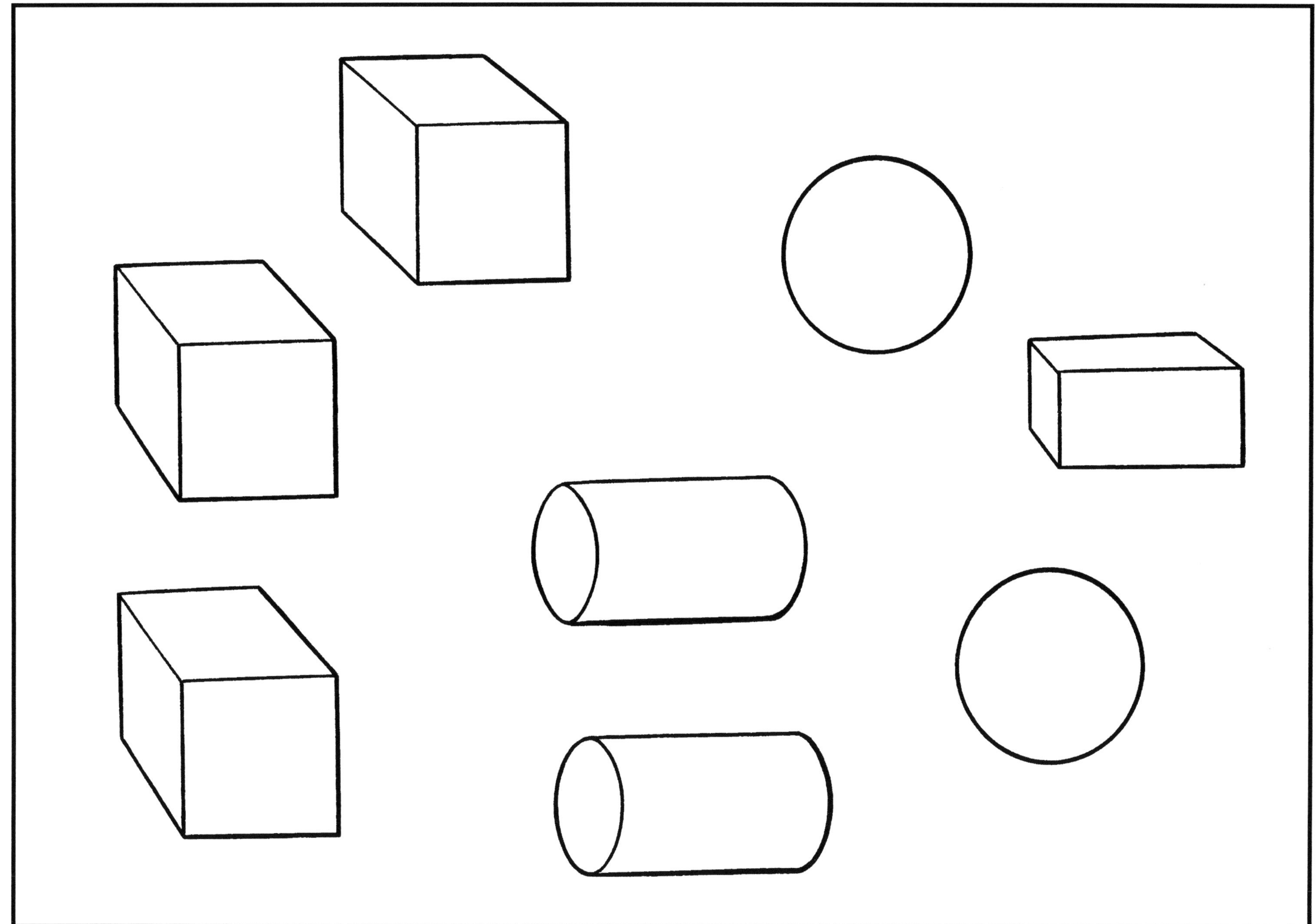

Making doodles

Start with a simple shape.

Add to it. You could use handwriting patterns, dots, single- or cross-hatching.

The doodle should grow slowly.
Draw as carefully as you can.

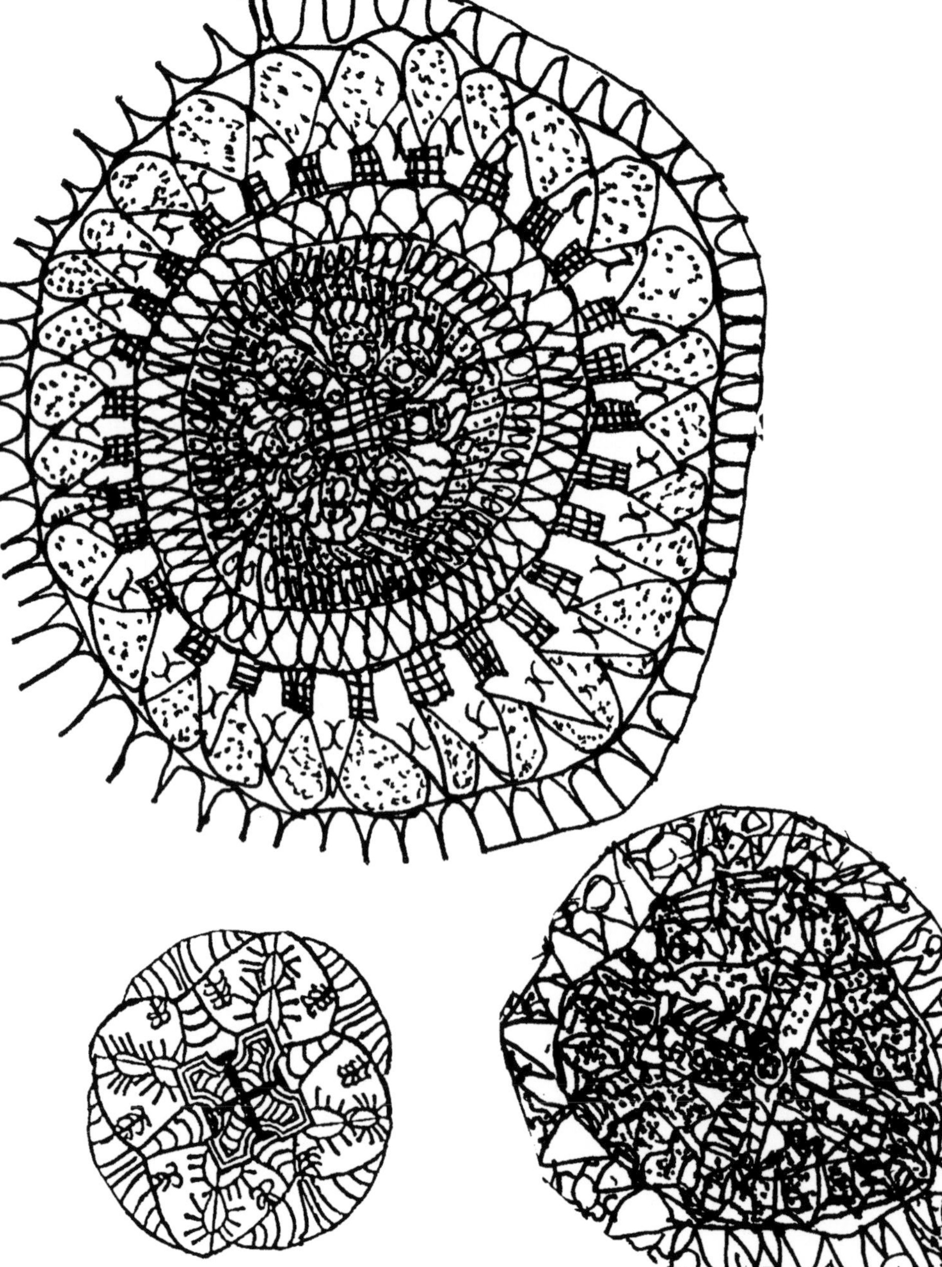

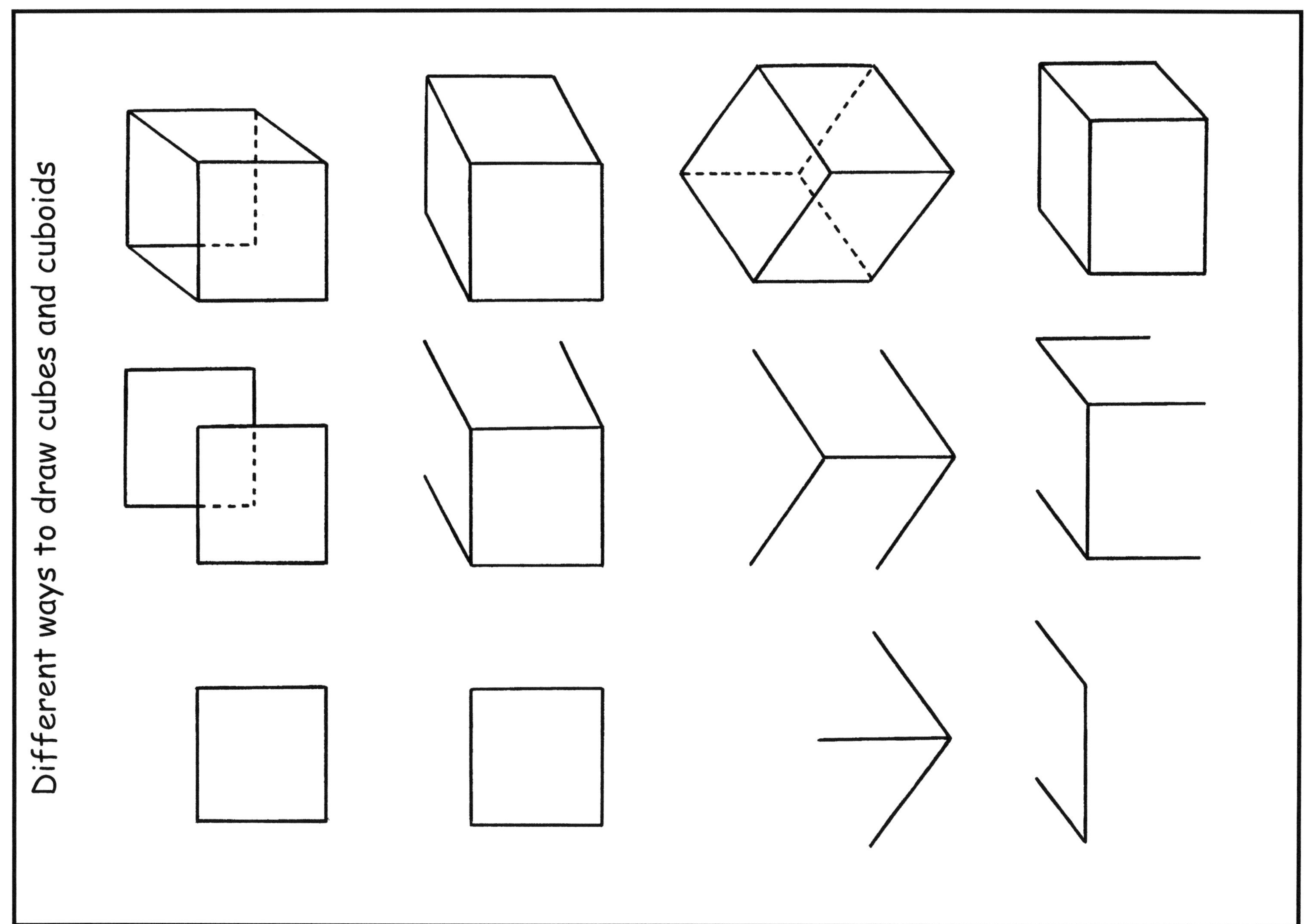
Different ways to draw cubes and cuboids

Et c'est logique que tu y ailles puisque moi
je ne puis être sûr que la famille reste
au même endroit cette année (cependant
elles y viennent depuis plusieurs années et
Perrichot doit connaître l'adresse en ville)
C'est peut être une illusion que je me
fais mais – je ne puis m'empêcher
d'y penser et peutêtre cela leur fera plaisir
et à toi aussi si tu les connais.
Ecoutes – je ferai tout mon possible
de t'envoyer de nouveaux dessins
pour Dordrecht
J'ai fait cette semaine deux natures
mortes.

toile de 30

une cafetière en fer emaillé bleu une tasse (à gauche) bleu
de roi et or un pot à lait carrelé bleu pâle & blanc
une tasse – à droite blanche à dessins bleu & orangé sur
une assiette de terre jaune gris un pot en barbotine
ou majolique bleu avec dessins rouges verts bruns
enfin 2 oranges et 3 citrons la table est couverte
d'une draperie bleue le fond est jaune vert
donc 6 bleus différents et 4 ou 5 jaunes & orangés
L'autre nature morte est le pot de majolique avec des
fleurs sauvages

'Still life drawing' (from sketchbook) by Vincent van Gogh

'Reading with Globe' by Michael Craig-Martin

'Plant Pot by Patrick Caulfield
© The Estate of Patrick Caulfield 2005.
All Rights Reserved, DACS

Guidelines for drawing figures

- ❒ You can fit about 5–6 heads into a child's body (6–7 into an adult's body).
- ❒ The middle of the body is the hip line (not the waist).
- ❒ Arms (when hanging down) end half way down the thighs.
- ❒ The shoulders are at least twice the width of the face.
- ❒ Necks are slightly narrower than heads.
- ❒ Foot length is similar to head length.

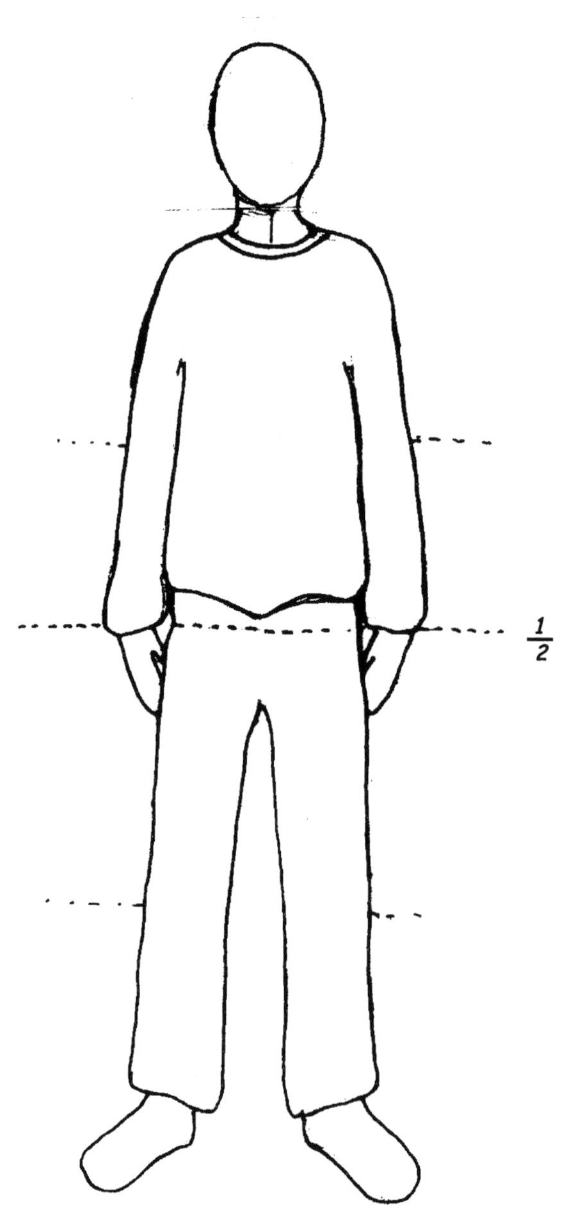

Guidelines for drawing faces

- ❒ From the front, heads are roughly oval.
- ❒ Faces vary in shape, some are more square, some more pointed, some more rounded.
- ❒ Eyes are almond shaped.
- ❒ Eyelashes grow out of eyelids.
- ❒ Eyes come half way down the face.
- ❒ The pupils are in line with the corners of the mouth.
- ❒ The base of the nose is half way between the eyes and the chin.
- ❒ The mouth is roughly half way between the base of the nose and the chin.
- ❒ You can rarely see the whole iris.
- ❒ The line between the lips is the darkest.
- ❒ Tops of ears are level with eyebrows.
- ❒ Hairline starts below the top of the head (unless the model is balding!).

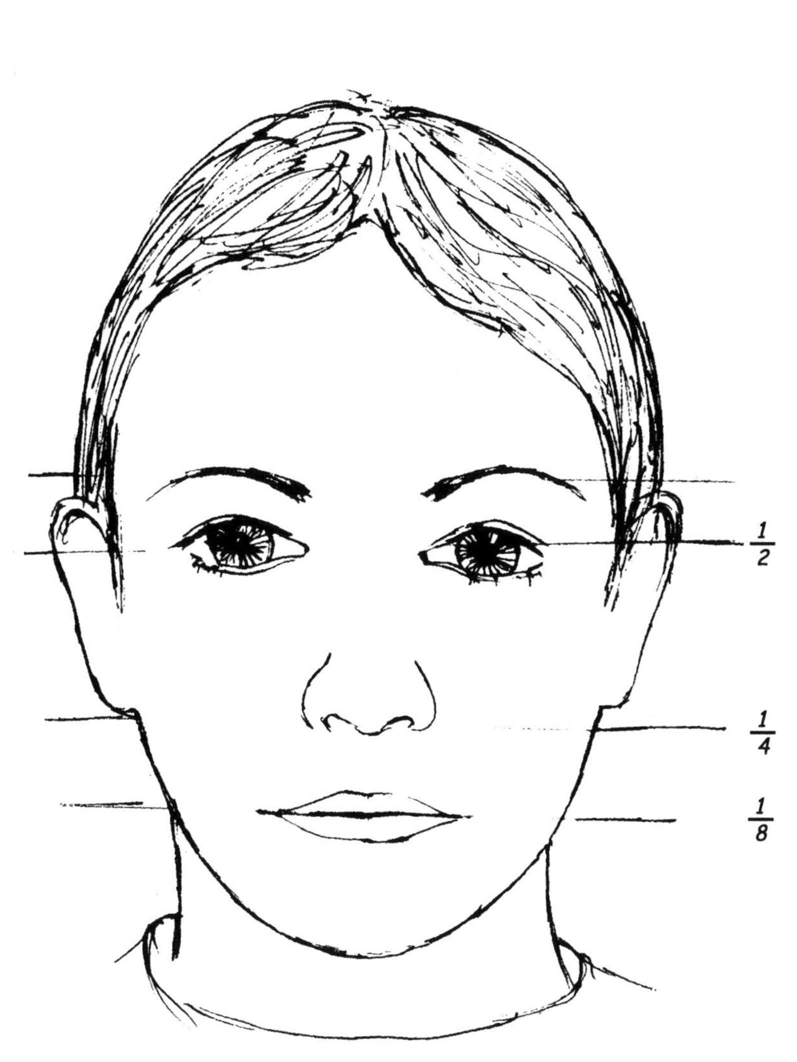

Drawing skills assessment list

Name:
Class:

Colour coding
Green = excellent
Yellow = satisfactory
Red = problems

Using media:

Draws using a range of marks with pencil
Draws in pen with confidence
Blends chalk and charcoal effectively

Use of key elements

Uses a variety of lines
Includes several tones
Depicts textures effectively
Observes and draws patterns

Strategies

Uses light lines at outset of drawing
Marks out main framework of drawing at the outset

Observation

During drawing, spends at least 30% of time looking, 70% drawing
Observes and includes detail
Draws subject reasonably accurately

Composition

Places subject well on paper
Uses space well

Speaking and self-evaluating skills

Talks effectively about own drawings
Identifies areas for development
Talks about works of art using appropriate vocabulary
Changes and improves drawing without prompting

Attitude

Draws with confidence
Concentrates well

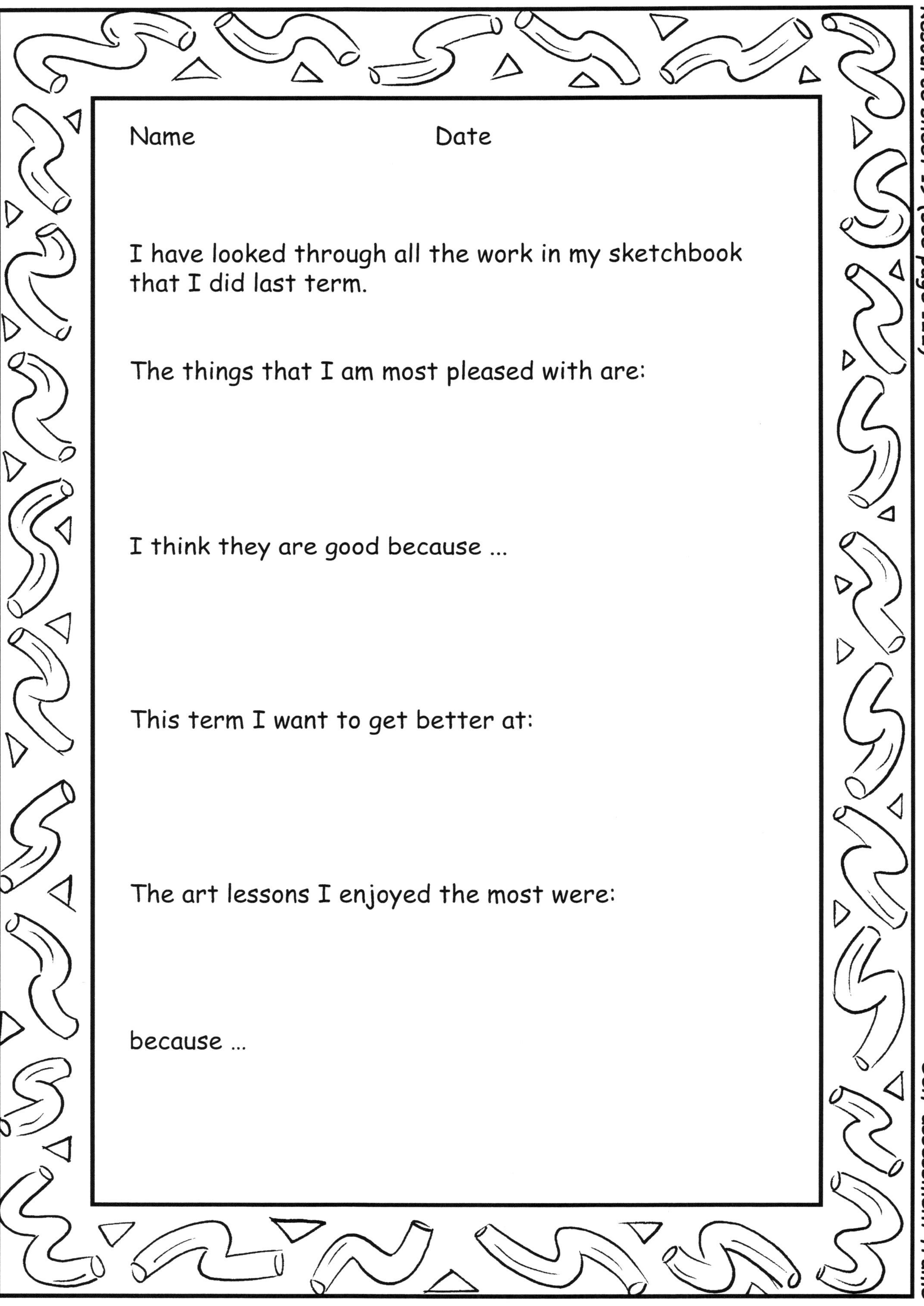

Name Date

I have looked through all the work in my sketchbook that I did last term.

The things that I am most pleased with are:

I think they are good because ...

This term I want to get better at:

The art lessons I enjoyed the most were:

because ...

Great art ideas for 3-12 year olds

Preschool Art

It's the Process, not the Product

With over 230 process-oriented, open-ended art experiences for children aged 3–6 in this book, you'll never be stuck for ideas.

Why not try something different?

Activities range from drawing, painting and sculpture to craft, collage and construction, including:

❒ Great goop ❒ Fingerpaint leaves ❒ Weaving board
❒ Corn-cob print ❒ Life-size animal ❒ Colourful stir sticks
❒ Towel chalk design ❒ Roller fence painting

The Big Messy* Art Book

**But Easy To Clean Up*

Open the door for children to explore art on a grander, more expressive scale. Suitable for all ages.

Go beyond the ordinary and into the amazing!

Activities range from drawing, painting and sculpture to craft, collage and construction. Each activity is labelled to indicate experience level required, amount of mess produced, ease of preparation and planning and any safety issues.

Activities include:
❒ living pendulum art ❒ doormat prints ❒ drip and fold with a friend
❒ squeegee scraping ❒ streamers artwork ❒ hanging glue squiggles
❒ fly swatter painting and much more ...

Discovering Great Artists

Hands-on Art for Children in the Styles of the Great Masters

Help children to understand and experience artists' styles and techniques through their own artistic works. Over 100 innovative, fun and unique art activities. Suitable for children aged 4–12. More than 80 great masters are featured ranging from Leonardo da Vinci and Renoir to Escher and Grandma Moses.

Activities include:
❒ Michelangelo – Fresco Plaque ❒ Rembrandt – Shadowy Faces
❒ Degas – Resist in Motion ❒ Picasso – Fractured Friend
❒ Lichtenstein – Comic Dots

Creative Activities for the Early Years

Thematic Art and Music Activities

Creative Activities for the Early Years contains over 160 art and craft activities for use by reception classes, nurseries, playgroups and mother and toddler groups, as well as by parents and carers.

These tried and tested activities will help children to:
❒ Use their imagination
❒ Express themselves creatively
❒ Communicate their ideas
❒ Develop gross and fine motor skills

The activities are grouped by popular early years themes, together with songs and rhymes, suggestions for stories and things to talk about. Whether your topic is the autumn, the Chinese New Year, the coastline, or ourselves, you can be sure you and your children will find the variety of activities interesting and entertaining.